TAROT
for
Self-transformation

TAROT
for
Self-transformation

Your journey to
happiness mapped out

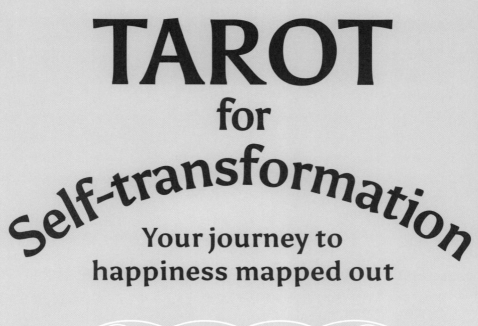

SAHAR HUNEIDI-PALMER

SIRIUS

To my stepdaughters Caroline and Olivia Palmer, and my nieces
Tamara, Nadine and Lana Al-Huneidi, and Yara, Tara and Nour
Kashlan; may you live as fiercely and courageously as The Fool did
and never shy away from a rewarding life experience!

PICTURE CREDITS:
Rider-Waite-Smith tarot deck images copyright Arcturus Publishing,
all other images courtesy of Shutterstock.

SIRIUS

This edition published in 2022 by Sirius Publishing, a division of
Arcturus Publishing Limited,
26/27 Bickels Yard, 151–153 Bermondsey Street,
London SE1 3HA

ISBN: 978-1-3988-2046-3
AD008721UK

Printed in China

Contents

Introduction

Tarot is one of the most popular and complex systems of divination used today. Hidden within its images and symbols is centuries-old knowledge of the ancient philosophers of classical Greece – the mystics who influenced the teachings of 14th-century clergy, who themselves departed from the beliefs of the state church to find spiritual understanding. Although their studies were conducted in secret, their ideas nevertheless influenced the latter-day scholars who founded the western esoteric schools of enlightenment. By the 18th century, tarot was regarded as a tool to preserve and express this secret, or sacred, knowledge – the path to self-awareness and enlightenment told through the journey of The Fool.

The Fool

The Fool – the first of the tarot cards, which is numbered zero – attains wisdom through the trials and tribulations of life. On his journey, The Fool awakens and matures. We see him changed at the end of his quest, standing tall in The World (which is the last card of this transformative journey), having attained mastery of mystical knowledge.

Tarot, as we know it today, originated in ninth-century China as playing cards. Along the way, many cultures and civilisations added to the arrangement of the deck before it was established as a divination tool centuries later (we'll explore that further in the following section). This book focuses on using the tarot as a self-help tool for insights and guidance that will help you live better and deepen your understanding of how to transform your life.

To illustrate this transformative journey of The Fool, we have chosen the Rider-Waite-Smith deck because its rich imagery and symbolism, which includes numbers, characters, astrology and events, make it an ideal deck for the beginner as well as the seasoned reader. Since its creation in 1909, the Rider-Waite-Smith has become one of the most popular tarot decks and a template for many others.

Originally known as the Rider-Waite pack, it was created by Arthur Edward Waite, a US-born British poet and scholarly mystic. It was subsequently renamed to acknowledge the contribution of the artist who designed it – Pamela Colman Smith, a British artist, illustrator, writer, publisher and occultist. Smith's innovative and detailed illustrations of the minor cards were a significant departure from previous tarot decks, which were principally based on the Tarot of Marseilles, popular in France in the 17th and 18th centuries.

In numbering the major arcana cards, this book follows the numbering assigned in the Tarot of Marseilles, which is to say the Justice Card is 8, and the Strength card 11 (pages 62 and 65, respectively).

Divination and self-awareness

Divination is about seeking guidance that helps you navigate your life and gain deeper insights into creating a better future. Keep in mind that no one knows the future, and nothing is written in stone. What the cards indicate is a trajectory, if you like, taking in your current situation, your present state of mind, your history, the obstacles that stand in your way and what you need to understand to clear them.

The tarot provides you with a creative, visual way to reflect on your life and inspire you with out-of-the-box solutions. It also helps you to see matters from a different perspective, and perhaps even to take actions and decisions to create a brighter future. It could be compared to a compass that helps you to chart your journey and navigate safely until you reach your destination or desired goals. Without a compass, one can miss the big picture, the right turns and exits, or lose sight of the destination completely.

When interpreting the tarot cards, you are using your intuition – that innate ability we all have but which is more fully developed in some people than in others. Practice, however, will improve it. Moreover, it might encourage you to know that according to cognitive scientists, one of the main functions of our brain is to predict the future to preserve our survival: we are designed to perceive a situation, learn from past experiences and predict a desirable outcome. Learning the tarot cards can enhance your perspective and understanding as it brings both halves of the

*"You are the secret.
Let tarot guide you.
And remember, if you
want to embody
The World card, first
you must ask for it."*

*Sasha Graham –
Contemporary author*

brain together. The intuitive, creative side is unlocked by the beautifully illustrated cards – rich with colour, numbers and symbols – and the logical half responds to the information on each card, its meaning and interpretation.

When tarot cards are laid out in a spread together, intuition and knowledge help you to weave a story, develop a perspective on your situation, and to see patterns more clearly which otherwise may not be obvious. As a result, the tarot can help you to gain insights and develop a deeper understanding so you can make better decisions to create a life you enjoy.

The origins of the tarot

The origins of the tarot are as enigmatic as the cards themselves, but they started their journey as playing cards in China during the Tang Dynasty around ninth century AD as the result of woodblock technology. The cards didn't include numbers or pictures and were played with dice to entertain the royal house. Later on, they were used as 'play money' cards, much like Monopoly money.

By the 15th century, a 38-card deck existed, divided into four suits, all related to money (coins, strings of coins and so on). Later, two more suits were added featuring characters from a famous Chinese novel, *Water Margin*, marking their rank and suit. By now, you can see the beginnings of the images on the major cards; the minor cards suits originated with the coin, or the pentacle.

Playing cards for 'trick-taking' games became very popular and spread from China throughout Asia. They reached the Islamic Mamluk Sultanate, which ruled Egypt, the Levant and the Hijaz (western Arabia) from the mid-13th to the early 16th centuries. Every culture added to the playing cards. A complete deck, known as the Topkapi, was discovered in 1939 near Istanbul, dating back to the 15th century. It contained 52 cards comprising four suits: polo-sticks, coins, swords and cups. Each suit contained ten pip (or numeral) cards and three court cards, called malik (king), nā'ib malik (viceroy or deputy king) and thānī nā'ib (second or under-deputy). No pictures were included yet, but there were abstract designs on the cards.

Most likely, playing cards entered Europe through Egypt's Mamluk Empire. The earliest record of them in Europe was found near the city of Bern in 1367, during a crackdown on card games. Their popularity was viewed as a social plague: a Dominican preacher referred to them as 'the devil's instrument' – which was the first reference to the much feared – and misunderstood – card, The Devil.

The cards then progressed through several variations as they spread across Europe. In the late 14th century, Europeans used the tarot for the entertainment of the aristocracy. The Mamluk court cards were changed to represent European royalty and their attendants. Religious images were added, such as angels (presented in Temperance, The Lovers and Judgement) and the Pope (The Hierophant and Death cards). The Devil was probably added to deter the populace from the 'evils of idle play'. That's how popular the tarot cards were!

The word tarot is thought to have been derived from the Italian name of the card game, *tarocchi*. During the 17th century, the tarot underwent further modifications to include Arabic numerals. Picture cards became known as face cards and included titles. In Italy, papal images were added, and the lower rank-cards became known as pip cards to differentiate them from the face cards.

Until then, the tarot was strictly for playing card games. However, around 1788–9, the first tarot deck specifically designed for occult purposes, containing themes relating to ancient Egypt, was given the name Etteilla. Antoine Court de Gébelin, a French clergyman, wrote: 'Tarot was not merely a game of cards but was in fact of ancient Egyptian origin, of mystical Qabalistic import, and of deep divine significance.' There is no evidence of this as the ancient Egyptian language had not yet been deciphered at the time, but the belief in such a connection endured and, after Court de Gébelin's writings, the tarot began to adopt a divinatory role.

In 1850, French authors such as Boiteau d'Ambly and Jean-Alexandre Vaillant started to promote the idea that tarot cards had been brought to Europe by the Romani. The late 1880s saw the spread of occult tarot in Europe and the rise of several esoteric schools of thought. By the close of the 19th century, tarot was widely regarded as being rooted in occult and mysticism. Éliphas Lévi Zahed, a French esotericist and poet, who started out as a clergyman in the Catholic church, wrote more than 20 books about magic, Kabbalah, alchemical studies and occultism in the 19th century. Among them, *The Book of Hermes* – in addition to other influences – led to the birth of the Hermetic Order of Golden Dawn, a secret society devoted to the study and practice of the occult, metaphysics and paranormal activities, of which Arthur Edward Waite, creator of the Rider-Waite-Smith deck, was a member. Lévi claimed that the tarot existed before Moses and was, in fact, a universal key of erudition, philosophy, and magic that could unlock Hermetic and Kabbalistic concepts.

This brings us to the tarot deck of choice for this book. When he commissioned her to illustrate his deck, Waite gave Pamela Colman Smith detailed instructions for each card, telling her to add Hebrew letters, elemental and planetary signs. Colman Smith and Waite were both former members of the the Hermetic Order of Golden Dawn and influenced by Lévi and other French occult revivalists who were guided, in turn, by the philosophers of classical Greece, such as Pythagoras, who theorised mathematical concepts, assigning numbers to geometric shapes, music and planetary motion. Although, as a game deck, the tarot was already numbered, the vibrational meaning of the numbers and the symbols assigned to the deck created by Rider-Waite-Smith were inspired by the studies of Pythagoras (for more on numerology, see Chapter Three, which begins on page 76).

Michael Dummett, one of the most significant British philosophers of the last century and a scholar in card-game history, wrote: 'Without the tarot, the magic of the ancients is a closed book.' This magic is now in your hands. Let the cards speak to you and you will discover what they mean as you fire up your imagination and intuition.

The tarot deck

A standard tarot deck features 78 cards divided into two groups: the first includes 22 major cards, known as the major arcana ('greater secrets'). They are numbered from 0 to 21 and reflect important life changes, milestones, lessons, events, and people. The second group comprises the 56 minor cards, or minor arcana ('lesser secrets'), which give more detailed information, with descriptions and sometimes timings, as well as day-to-day-events. The minor cards are arranged in four suits – Wands, Cups, Swords and Pentacles. Each suit has a ruling element and corresponds to a specific aspect. Wands correspond to fire and action. Cups symbolise water and emotions. Swords represent air and relate to the intellect and decisions. Pentacles represent earth, money and achievement.

Minor cards are also numbered from ace to 10, in addition to four court cards in each suit: King, Queen, Knight and Page. Court cards represent a person, reflecting their characteristics, age, status, abilities, traits and state of mind. You will notice the similarity between the minor cards of the tarot and a traditional deck of playing cards.

Tarot cards with a picture of a person can represent you, people in your life, or whoever you are reading for. The enquirer refers to the person who is consulting the tarot cards, or the person on whose behalf you are consulting them. More details on the minor cards are provided in the section overleaf, *What makes a good tarot reader* (page 12).

Tarot and intuition

The rich imagery on the tarot cards helps activate your intuition and imagination as you gaze upon them. Each card has its own meaning, as well as a contextual meaning, according to its position in a spread. We'll look more closely at the individual meaning of each card and spread later in this book.

As you connect with the cards, the symbols and illustrations will help you to think out of the box and receive guidance. When the cards are laid out in a spread, they appear to tell a story which can offer deeper insights into any situation you enquire about. If you like, the tarot can help you 'see' aspects around a situation that you are not clear about. The cards provide an opportunity to step back and look at a situation from a different angle.

This creative visual process is not only fun, but also helps to enhance your imagination and intuition, as well as your ability to gain a different perspective by developing your personal awareness. The cards can also help you to find and understand what your life purpose is, as you will discover later in the chapter on numerology and Your Personal Tarot Profile (pages 76 and 97 respectively).

By uncovering the symbology, mythology and numerology of the tarot, the meaning of each card and its interpretation, in combination with others and in the context of where it falls in a spread, you will have a treasure trove of information. You will become aware of the blocks and patterns that need to be changed to make improvements in your life. The tarot is truly an invaluable tool in personal guidance and development.

You will also learn more about yourself and why you create what you attract in your life, your strengths and weaknesses, as well as what your date of birth represents – your soul's purpose. Understanding numerology provides you with insights to capitalise on and teaches you to express your innate abilities and essence – who you truly are as consciousness or energy. Learning how all these different aspects are interconnected will help you rise up to meet the various challenges you encounter. Along your journey, you become more buoyant, bounce back quickly from setbacks and continue to fulfil your life's purpose.

What makes a good tarot reader?

You are your greatest asset. The tarot cards went through a journey of several hundred years: each culture and school of thought added to their meaning and the way they are interpreted, and when you get to connect with and know the cards, you will be doing the same. Each card will reveal its meaning to you, and you will discover new interpretations and insights as you progress.

Three aspects will allow you to grow and become a good reader, or consultant, of the tarot:

- ∞ Your intention
- ∞ Your curiosity to learn something new
- ∞ How often you practise

Intention

By setting your intention, you are creating context for the information you are about to tap into and perceive. This will lead you to a better interpretation as the cards weave a story which you will interpret accordingly (see the section on how to phrase questions on page 102). If your intention is to receive guidance, then it will happen. On the other hand, if your intention is to control or avoid any changes, you might fail. The only constant in life is change – we can only control how we respond to such changes as they unfold.

Here's a suggestion: hold yourself accountable for everything you say and everything you do. Accountability is empowering, as The Fool's journey will demonstrate. This self-awareness will strengthen you – like a lightning rod, you will become a clear conduit for guidance and your intuition will grow.

So, what is your intention? Write it below, without thinking too much. Remember that you want to tap into your inner sense of knowing.

INTENTION:

....

....

Curiosity

When you maintain a curious mindset, your mind is open to receiving new knowledge. Like our hero, The Fool, you will start with a blank canvas and allow the bigger picture to emerge. Stay curious and keep working on developing yourself. Read books, take courses or meditate. Bear in mind that very often when we learn something new, the logical side of the brain will fight any fresh way of thinking because it perceives it as a threat to what we already know. By keeping an open mind, your intuition will flow and your experience will be a rewarding and a pleasurable one.

Practice

Finally, the old adage 'practice makes perfect' applies here. With practice you will be able to form a bond with the cards and communicate better with them. You will also notice that the information will flow into your mind more easily. You will begin to see patterns, or combinations of cards, that speak to you too.

When you start consulting your tarot cards, it will be normal to refer to this book and check the meaning of each card. However, with practice, your understanding will deepen and your interpretations will become clearer. You will develop your own dictionary of interpretation and gradually you will probably refer less to this book, and more to your own notes. You can keep a special journal just for those notes.

What is a tarot reading?

A tarot reading is a combination of three elements:
- ∞ you, as the reader, and your psychic ability;
- ∞ knowledge of the card meanings and how to interpret them;
- ∞ interpretation of a tarot card spread.

You, as the reader

You will become a better reader by practising. You are like our hero, The Fool, starting from zero and going on a psychic adventure. So, do not be afraid to make a *Fool* of yourself!

Having a ritual will develop and ground your psychic ability, or intuition. Establish your ritual and follow it at the beginning of each reading. It will help you to be an objective reader, open to receiving new information.

So, set a time aside when you are not distracted and have a journal handy. Keep a record of all your insights and document your own journey as you go through this book. Clear your mind by taking few breaths and let go of any expectation. You can also light a tea candle, and focus your attention on the flame for a few moments to clear your mind.

Infinity exercise to trigger your intuition

The following simple exercise will help you develop crystal clear intuition: start by drawing an infinity figure with your dominant hand, in your tarot journal and, as close as possible to the initial drawing, go over it until you feel at ease with it. Next, hold the pen with your other hand (your non-dominant one), and try to trace over that outline, staying as close as possible to the original infinity shape you first drew.

When you feel comfortable with that, hold the pen with both hands and return to the infinity figure, staying close to the lines you drew previously. The objective here is NOT speed, but focus. Repeat each step about 10 times.

You can make this part of your routine and use it every time before you consult the tarot. The infinity exercise enhances your intuition and allows both halves of the brain to work together in synergy.

Figure 1

Brain-sync exercise

There are many exercises that help synchronise both brain hemispheres when learning something new. Generally speaking, the left hemisphere deals with linear, logical, practical learning and the right with non-linear intuitive or abstract learning. Use the following brain-sync exercise before you begin any learning task. With repetition, it enhances mind-body integration and reduces cognitive anxiety. It also maximises your brain's ability by syncing both halves together, boosting your potential in a very short time too.

Sit quietly in a chair, with your back straight and your body relaxed. Cross your right ankle over your left. Now extend both arms in front of you, with your palms facing each other. Cross your right wrist over the left and twist your hands so that your palms touch, interlace your fingers and put your right thumb over the left.

With your hands still clasped together, fold your arms in towards your heart, with the elbows facing down. Tuck your ankles under the seat. Close your eyes and breathe in a relaxed, natural way until you find your own comfortable breathing rhythm. You can choose to listen to relaxing music and burn your favourite essential oil to further enhance this exercise.

SEVEN TIPS FOR DEVELOPING
CLEAR GUIDANCE

1

Establish your own routine and stick to it. Routines give you structure and help you develop your intuition steadily and accurately.

2

Inspire to empower. Keep it real – do not look for drama or phenomena. Never try to scare, dramatise or introduce fear, doubt or worry into your mind or that of others, if you are conducting a reading for someone you know.

3

Look after yourself and you will be looked after. If intuition is not developed in a healthy manner, psychic work can be very draining and may affect your wellbeing. So, sleep well, eat healthily and drink lots of water to remain replenished (we are walking batteries, so water will help 'circulate' and regulate steady energy flow).

4

Keep a tarot journey journal. Maintain a record of your journey of transformation as you learn the tarot. A few suggestions are offered in the following section.

5

Integrate your knowledge. Keep a dream journal and monitor how your dreams change – it will help you to get to know who *you* are. As your knowledge grows, your perception expands and this will be reflected in the quality of your dreams as your conscious integrates with your subconscious.

6

Keep your ego in check. Be true to yourself! The accuracy of a reading comes from maintaining your integrity while you work with the tarot. Set your intention, breathe deeply, meditate and keep an open mind free from any preconceived ideas or expectations. A reader is like a conduit for receiving information. The more you keep your conduit well maintained and clean, the clearer your interpretations will be.

7

Hold yourself accountable. Accountability will help you stay in alignment, and empower you too. Be mindful of everything you say and do. Whenever you are not clear about interpreting a tarot reading, ask yourself: 'What does this mean?' or 'What is it showing me?' Your intuition will let you know. Do not be afraid to lose credibility by saying: 'I'm not sure what this means.' Making up an interpretation, or providing a negative one, will compromise your integrity.

Keep growing! As a tarot reader, you are a conduit for guidance. The better the vessel, the more accurate and clear that guidance is. Keep up your personal development, and stay curious by developing your talents and abilities.

Getting to know the tarot

The tarot is a tool that helps you deepen your connection with your inner guidance. When more than one card is laid out in a sequence, it is known as a spread. Together, the cards weave a story that triggers your imagination and intuition. Guidance comes through the story the cards tell. This book will you help you uncover and interpret the guidance you seek.

Tarot card spreads

As noted above, using a combination of more than two tarot cards is referred to as a spread. The story told by the cards combines two aspects: the individual meaning of a card, as well as its interpretation according to where it falls within a spread. You can develop your own spreads as you become more proficient with the tarot. However, by learning a few simple spreads that use major cards only, such as a yes-or-no spread, a three-card spread, or a five-card spread, you can receive clear, quick guidance. For example, in a three-card spread the template would be: past, present and future. Or it might be background, current circumstances and result/ outcome. So each card will have an individual meaning, as well as an interpretation according to its location.

For deeper insights and an overview of future trends, more complex and detailed spreads are used. For example, the 12-house astrological spread, in which tarot cards are laid out according to the astrological houses. This more complex spread combines astrology and the numerology of each tarot card (see Chapter Three on numerology, beginning page 76).

Begin by only using the major cards in a spread, as they will provide you with the main influences. Afterwards, you can start to combine the major cards with the minor, which supply more details and, often, timing. In this instance, lay out the major cards first, then shuffle and randomly choose the minor cards, after reversing five cards. A tarot spread, therefore, acts as a template that helps you interpret the cards within the context of the guidance you seek. We will look at spreads more closely in Chapter Four.

Reversed meaning of tarot cards

The tarot cards have their way of drawing your attention to what you need to become aware of. When you lay them out in a spread, there will always be a card that jumps out at you to deliver a message. The cards that are most feared are The Devil, Death, and probably Judgement too! However, the images are dramatic to convey an important transformative message that shouldn't be missed or ignored: for example, you are stuck in a situation you have outgrown, your emotions are getting the better of you, or a phase has to end to bring about the next step of your personal evolution.

Sometimes, events foretold are not so dramatic, but you still need to pay attention to them as they represent a significant turning point. One way of making such turning points apparent is to reverse two major cards and five minor cards when you are shuffling at the start of a reading (for more about reversing cards, see Chapter Four, page 100).

In some instances, cards that seem ominous have a more positive meaning when they appear reversed in a reading, such as The Hanged Man. Reversed, this card indicates the end of a waiting period. The Devil reversed indicates that you are about to be freed from bondage; Death reversed indicates your inability to accept the changes you are going through; and Judgement reversed denotes that you are going through an essential transformation and there is nothing that you can do about it!

CHAPTER ONE

Overview of the tarot cards

Learning the tarot can be a daunting experience, but don't let that put you off. This book will guide you through a clear and enjoyable path.

There are several layers to interpreting a tarot spread, referred to as a reading. Get to know the major cards first, because they are the foundation of self-awakening. Start by separating the major cards from the minor ones. When you feel more confident, you can start using the whole deck. Fortunately, the minor cards in the Rider-Waite-Smith deck are almost self-explanatory – you will understand them just by observing their evocative illustrations.

Knowing the traditional meaning of each of the major cards will give you a solid foundation and the confidence to get started. However, building on this knowledge by using your imagination will make your readings more accurate and relevant to you. If you are a seasoned tarot reader, take a fresh a look at the cards, try to let go of previous knowledge you may have. You may just discover new interpretations.

So, let's start now. Unpack your tarot deck, hold the cards between your hands, and shuffle well, in one direction, to absorb the energy of the cards. Next, hold the deck over your heart and ask for clear guidance every time you use them. Check out the guidance invocation at the beginning of the Chapter Four (page 100), or make up your own. Next, lay the cards on a table with the pictures facing you. Let your imagination guide you as you start dividing the cards in two groups: the first is for cards that

> "Life is a journey that must be travelled no matter how bad the roads and accommodations."
>
> Oliver Goldsmith – Poet (1728–1774)

have one person who dominates the image and has a title; the second group is for all the remaining images.

What is the main difference between the two groups?

GROUP ONE:

....

....

GROUP TWO:

....

....

Major cards

Now take a look at the first group of cards. Most of the 'people' cards in the first group, have either a title or a description of the person, such as The Magician, The Hanged Man or Strength, or are royal court cards such as King, Queen, Knight and Page. The former are major cards and the court cards fall into the minor arcana. In the main, pictures of people with a title represent descriptions, as well qualities, skills, talents or abilities, of people who come up in a tarot reading.

The major cards are the foundation of the tarot. They represent the journey of personal transformation, enlightenment and self-awakening. They also describe a significant person, phase, change or a transition in one's life. To begin with, use the major cards on their own when drawing a daily card for guidance, or for short-term or quick insights (see the section on tarot card spreads on pages 108-121). When it comes to a longer-term consultation, such as a New Year or birthday reading, more complex layouts, such as the 12-house astrological spread (see page 115), are appropriate and require the entire tarot deck. Using both major and minor cards together in a reading gives multi-layered information: detailed insights, relevant conditions and timings.

From imagination to intuition

Now get ready to exercise your imagination further and spark off your intuition! Select the major cards only, shuffle and spread them in front you with the images facing you. Reflect on them for a few minutes, and then divide them into eight groups – whichever way you feel.

There are no right or wrong answers, let your inner senses guide you. Focus on each group, one at a time, and describe what it represents to you, or why you placed those cards together. Your initial insights are important. Remember to write down your observations as this will help you develop clear insights later on when you do readings.

IMAGINATION EXERCISE 1		
GROUP	CARDS IN GROUP	YOUR REASONS FOR GROUPING
1		
2		
3		

IMAGINATION EXERCISE 1 (CONT.)		
4		
5		
6		
7		
8		

Figure 2a

Once you are done, contemplate the suggested groupings in Figure 2b overleaf, and see how it compares with your own. You can choose to repeat this imagination exercise at any time, but whichever way you are inspired to group the cards each time, you will certainly notice something new that you didn't see before. Repeating this exercise helps you to connect with each card more deeply, to uncover new, more meaningful interpretations and to develop your own tarot dictionary of interpretation.

IMAGINATION EXERCISE 2		
GROUP	CARDS IN GROUP	REASONS FOR POSSIBLE GROUPING
1	The Fool The World	Cardsofbeginningandendoftransformation.
2	The High Priestess The Hierophant	Both belong to spiritual institutions and wear spiritual clothes.
3	The Magician The Empress	Both have similar colours, with lots of roses, both seem to express abundance.
4	Temperance The Lovers	Both have an angel with wings.
5	The Sun The Moon The Stars	Stellar/celestial images.
6	The Hermit Strength	Attire is simpler, yet they seem to possess an intangible quality or ability.
7	The Emperor The Chariot Justice	Figures of authority, holding a staff, on a throne, in command.
8	The Hanged Man The Tower Wheel of Fortune The Devil Death Judgement	This group seems to be about changes or transformation, not just people – events that are happening suddenly, slowly or not at all.

Figure 2b

Minor cards

Most of the cards in this second group will depict 'people in situations'. They describe events or underlying conditions or required tools and skills to fulfil a goal. Often, the person in the image is holding a tool in his hands: namely, Pentacles (coins), Wands, Cups or Swords. The tool denotes the suit the card belongs to, and represents one of the elements of nature.

Minor cards are numbered from ace to 10 in a similar way to regular playing cards, where each suit also has four royal or court cards. Minor cards, including the court cards, also provide timings and influencing factors. To interpret a tarot reading, notice first which suit is dominant in a spread.

The best way to ease yourself into the minor cards is to lay out the cards in four rows, one for each suit, from ace to King, with the pictures facing you. Reflect on each suit separately by observing each illustration. Notice what every card evokes within you too. Here are a few elements to look for as you tune into each card or suit.

OVERALL IMPRESSION: What impression does each suit leave you with?

PEOPLE: What is your impression of the people illustrated (rich or poor, sad, happy or stressed)?

OBJECTS: What do you think the main object depicted in each suit represents as you look at the whole series?

ACTIVITY: What is the theme of the activity they are engaged in?

SURROUNDINGS: What is their surrounding environment like (land, water, abundant or arid and so on)?

Allow the answers to the above questions to surface in your mind, and keep a record of your observations in your journal regularly. Also jot down in your journal a brief description of what each suit represents to you, *before* you read on.

SUIT	ELEMENT	SEASON/ TIMING	KEYWORD
Wands	Fire	Spring	Ideas
Cups	Water	Summer	Emotions
Swords	Air	Autumn	Thoughts
Pentacles	Earth	Winter	Finance

INTERPRETATION/QUALITIES	CORRESPONDING PLAYING CARD SUIT
Male aspect, inspiration, renewal, manifestation of ideas, growth, communication and self-expression	♣
Female aspect, emotions, creativity, happiness, love, intuition, acceptance, flow	♥
Sharp mind, mental activity, intellect, logical thinking, decisions	♠
Money, material wealth, success, business, physical body, foundation, property	♦

Figure 3: A closer look at the minor card suits

The court cards

As you consider the court cards note the age, features and poise of each person, and note the object they are holding. That object represents the suit and indicates the element of nature, such as earth or water, to which that suit belongs.

Page of Wands

Knight of Wands

Queen of Wands

King of Wands

Page of Cups

Knight of Cups

Queen of Cups

King of Cups

Figure 4: The court cards

	KING	QUEEN	KNIGHT	PAGE
MEANING	Older man, authority, personality, vision, experience	Older woman, authority, personality, profession, enabler, creative	Young man, movement, action	Children, genre, timing
WANDS	Important, successful, kind, interested in business. Freckled, strawberry blond or brown hair	Capable and kind, practical. Brunette	Business-related travelling	Energetic
CUPS	Mature, caring, balanced, kind, in high position. Light hair/skin	Loving, helpful, intuitive. Fair	Loving sensitive person	Poetic, soft emotional
SWORDS	Powerful, professional, good mind, tough. Salt and pepper hair	Lonely, mentally sharp woman, who can overcome problems	Assertive man, moves quickly	Bright, difficult
PENTANGLES	Financial wizard, wealthy. Dark skin/hair	Abundant, helpful business woman. Dark skin/hair	Interested in money, methodical	Investment, laborious

Figure 5: Analysis of the court cards

The pip card numbers

Now look at the pip cards. How is the same number expressed in each suit? What similarities or differences do you notice? Try using one word to describe what each number represents below. For example, number 1 expresses beginnings.

NUMBER 1: . . . .

NUMBER 2: . . . .

NUMBER 3: . . . .

NUMBER 4: . . . .

NUMBER 5: . . . .

NUMBER 6: . . . .

NUMBER 7: . . . .

NUMBER 8: . . . .

NUMBER 9: . . . .

NUMBER 10: . . . .

NUMEROLOGY OF MINOR CARDS			
CARD		KEYWORDS	WANDS
ACE		New beginning	Inspiration, growth of an idea
2	II	Partnership, development	Choice of business partners
3	III	Outcome, expansion, collaboration, planning	Successful collaboration
4	IV	Stability	Enjoyable collaboration
5	V	Adjustment	Negotiation, competition
6	VI	Phases, steadying influences	Victorious achievement
7	VII	Several choices, disappointment, caution	Opposition from others
8	VIII	Justice, karma, organisation	Air travel, sudden movement
9	IX	Faith in self, fulfilment, integration	Need to be flexible, obstinate, afraid to lose status
10	X	Transformation, new cycle	Too much pressure

NUMEROLOGY OF MINOR CARDS		
CUPS	SWORDS	PENTACLES
Happiness, new relationship	Decision, strength to overcome an obstacle	Receiving large amount of money
Love affair, good friendship	Strained situation, decision between two alternatives	Balance, business partnership
Birth of a child, celebration	Emotional quarrels, separation	Skilled
Boredom	Rest is needed	Doing well financially
Disappointment or something good about to happen (depends on spread/other cards)	Unexpected difficult situation that can't be avoided	Serious financial problems
Reliving childhood memories, meeting old friends	Travel across water, away from troubles	Financial help
Daydreaming, vivid imagination, need to be realistic	Deception is likely, be cautious	Hard work is needed
Change of heart, moving in a new direction	Trapped conditions, stalemate	Skilled
Wishes come true, beneficial	Distress, mental stress or illness	Material success
Special happy event, marriage/children	Deception, treachery, stress leading to physical illness	Family money

Figure 6: Numerology reference table for the minor cards

Starting your tarot journey

A good way to begin is to get to know the tarot one card at a time. You will learn more quickly and easily when your journey is enjoyable. Here are a few examples of how to make learning more fun.

One-card day reading

At the beginning of your day, shuffle the cards as you ask yourself: 'What is today about?' Or, perhaps, 'How will my day go?' Pick one card and leave it face down on the table. At the end of the day, look at your card and then write a brief description of how the day went in your journal. Describe any significant happenings and see how they relate to the card you chose. Doing this daily will help you build your own tarot encyclopaedia.

One-card night reading

Another way to get to know the tarot is to pick one card before going to bed and place it under your pillow. Before you get out of bed the next morning, write down the card, and what feelings – or dreams – you woke up with. Keeping a record of your nightly explorations will develop your psychic ability.

Communicating with your cards

Did you know that imagination enhances intuition? Working with the major cards is a tool to facilitate your intuition. It is also a great way to trigger your imagination and understand the cards' meaning. Once you connect with the major cards, you will find it easier to acquaint yourself with the minor cards: you will spot similarities between images, variations on a theme, or might simply develop your own way of tuning into a card and letting the imagery speak to you.

Visualization

So, take a few deep breaths, pick up the deck and shuffle the cards stating your intention to receive clear guidance. Then, you can either randomly pick a card from your deck, or spread them out in front of you in a row, allowing a card to jump out at you. Hold that card between your hands and imagine that you are looking at a portrait painting or a snapshot of a person, location or situation. You can also lay it down in front you on a clear background away from all the other cards. Gaze at it for a while, then pick up a pen and start writing in your tarot journal. Record the name of the card and start to write a description of what the painting is. For example, let's say you are looking at The Hermit, you might start by writing down what is initially obvious.

'The picture is of an older man with a white beard. He is wearing a grey robe and hood. His head is down in humility as he stands alone, against a plain background holding a lantern in his right hand and a staff in his left. The light emitted by the lantern has the shape of a shining star. He is standing on rugged ground, which appears to be covered with snow. The number above his head is 9.'

When you feel that you have observed all the details in the picture, close your eyes and imagine that you are walking into it yourself. What do you feel? What do you see? What do you smell? What is the environment like? Do you hear any sounds? Is there anything else around? Is it hot or cold? What season is it? Use your five senses. Next, imagine talking to the figure in the picture: ask them who they are, what they represent, what they are doing, or anything else you wish to know. Close your eyes and jump into that picture now!

Slowly and gently, open your eyes and write down your impressions before you forget them. Finish your description by adding one word that identifies what this painting stands for. Congratulations – you have just started using your inner senses or, in other words, your intuition! In fact, you have done more than that – you have synced both halves of your brain: your logic and creative imagination. You can use this 'walking into a picture' exercise as a daily creative meditation practice.

In the above visualization, you grounded yourself in logic, by observing all the details on the card, which you could see with your own eyes. Once your brain was more relaxed and your intuition triggered, the creative side of your brain was ready to be put to use.

The following template, figure 7 overleaf, helps to uncover your personal interpretations. Start by describing the factual elements of a picture first, then allow your imagination to wander.

	CARD	The Fool	The Tower	Queen of Cups	Ten of Wands
MAIN IMAGE	Scene		✓		✓
	Character	✓		✓	
TYPE	Major	✓	✓		
	Minor			✓	✓
	Card Number	0	16 = 1 + 6 = 7	Court Card	10 = 1 + 0 = 1
	Other Symbols you Notice	On a precipice	Lightning	Feet in water	Can't see in front of him
	Keywords	New beginning	Sudden changes	Emotions	Man overloaded with responsibility
	Your Notes	Leaping into the unknown	Destruction of the old	A loving woman	Too many problems
	Suit			Cups	Wands

Figure 7: Building your knowledge of tarot cards

Tarot readings

Reading the tarot requires a spread, in which you lay out the cards and interpret their meaning according to where they fall. There are several templates for doing this. Templates can be simple, such as a three-card spread, or complex, for example, the 12-house astrological spread. In any spread you use either the major cards on their own or in combination with the minor cards. However, it is easier if you start with simple spreads, using major cards only, and then gradually build to using complex spreads as your confidence and knowledge grow.

Simple spreads are as important as complex ones. Each have their own purpose. Sometimes, you may require quick and clear guidance, such as a yes-or-no answer – in this case, go for a three-card spread. Other times, you may wish for more details, such as timings or upcoming trends, for which a 12-house spread is more appropriate.

For now, keep in mind that a tarot reading is a combination of the meaning of each individual card and its interpretation according to its location within a spread. Spreads add a layer of complexity to a reading. In a sense, they combine intuition with the logic of using a pre-constructed template, where each house or location has a pre-set meaning. Your intuition will interpret the cards according to the story told by their location in that template. With practice, your readings can give you practical advice.

The following table summarises the meaning of each of the major tarot cards. Compare the information below with your own notes.

CARD AND NUMBER	KEYWORDS	REVERSED MEANING	AFFIRMATION
0 – THE FOOL	New beginning, dissolution of ego, taking a risk	Foolishness, Bad risk	"I am ready to leap into the unknown."
1 – THE MAGICIAN	Enterprise, the initiator, disciplined learner	Confusion	"Within me are all the resources I need to realise my success."
2 – THE HIGH PRIESTESS	Inner senses, intuition, the unknown	Self-delusion	"I trust my inner senses to guide me one step at a time."

CARD AND NUMBER	KEYWORDS	REVERSED MEANING	AFFIRMATION
3 – THE EMPRESS	Abundance, birth, happiness	Limited abundance	"I am connected to earth at all times. Abundance is unlimited."
4 – THE EMPEROR	Judiciousness/ structure, authority	Foolishness	"I am my own authority. I create structures that I am accountable for."
5 – THE HIEROPHANT	Higher mind/ destiny, the oracle	Materialistic	"I make my own traditions. I express what I adopt in my own unique way."
6 – THE LOVERS	Partnerships, co-creating	Indecision	"Loving myself leads me to love."
7 – THE CHARIOT	Mastery victory, effort rewarded	Lack of control	"I transcend all obstacles and time. Inspiration guides me."
8 – JUSTICE	Fortitude, prudence, legal matters	Dissolution of agreements	"I am aware of the consequences of my actions, thoughts and intentions."
9 – THE HERMIT	Inner wisdom, seeker of knowledge/ teacher of higher wisdom	Introversion	"I operate from my higher, wiser mind."
10 – WHEEL OF FORTUNE	New cycle of cause and effect, unexpected change of circumstance	Bad cycle	"I go with the flow and accept changes that come my way."
11 – STRENGTH	Infinite integration of spirit and matter	Inability to control passions, Healing of self and others	"My inner strength is a gentle force. It enchants and heals all obstacles."
12 – THE HANGED MAN	Surrender, sacrifice	Useless sacrifice	"In stillness I find higher perspective."

CARD AND NUMBER	KEYWORDS	REVERSED MEANING	AFFIRMATION
13 – DEATH	Transformation, destroyer and creator of new structure, end/loss/rebirth	Fear of change	"I accept endings and welcome new beginnings."
14 – TEMPERANCE	Harmony through balance, conflict resolution	Imbalance	"In balance I realise harmony."
15 – THE DEVIL	Restriction, enslaved, obsession, lust	Beginning of flow	"I am the master of my emotions and desires."
16 – THE TOWER	Upheaval, destruction of the old	Disruptive behaviour	"I embrace destruction of the old and make way for the new"
17 – THE STAR	Illumination, bliss	Let go of doubt	"Awakened, I see the naked truth. Higher wisdom always guides me. The sky is the limit."
18 – THE MOON	Wisdom of the unconscious, illusion	Self-deception	"When my emotions confuse me, my subconscious guides me through my dreams."
19 – THE SUN	Joy, success	Success awaits	"My talents and abilities assure my success. I shine my light into the world in return."
20 – JUDGEMENT	Total transformation, reinvention, self-developmental turning point	Forced changes	"The choices I make every day, align me with my life's purpose."
21 – THE WORLD	Fulfilment, integration, expansion	Recognition awaits	"My labour, love and courage fulfil my ambition. I am recognised. The world is my oyster."

Figure 8: Quick reference table for major card

CHAPTER TWO
The Fool's journey

The Fool's journey is about individuating and finding our place in life. It is about expressing who we truly are, our talents and abilities in our unique way. Undergoing The Fool's journey helps us to realise our life's ambition and purpose by developing a greater and deeper awareness of how to direct our own 'movie' or story to create a fulfilling life. The journey shows us that not all of life's experiences are joyful – some are painful indeed, but they are also necessary for us to mature, individuate and gain wisdom by learning the lessons behind those experiences. We learn through The Fool's journey that understanding life's experiences gives us a new perspective, and therefore wisdom, which emotionally heals and, in turn, allows for new opportunities to emerge. Essentially, we can move forward in life with joy and ease.

And, just when The Fool thinks he has learnt all the lessons, he experiences even greater losses he is unprepared for. Yet, through enduring them, he transitions into deeper growth taking yet another leap into the unknown, into a new level of perception that enables him to reinvent his life anew. He uncovers his own personal resilience and reaches a level of self-mastery that helps him to maintain his alignment and manifest from spirit into the material world. At the end of his journey, The Fool is fulfilled. He has transformed into a wiser person who has mastered his instincts, emotions and mind.

Told through the major cards, the journey develops aspects of The Fool's personality – each time at a higher level of awareness. We meet the major cards as characters and experiences that shape The Fool's integrated growth: inner skills, knowledge, self-control and wisdom are gained through these cards.

> "The Fool is potentially everybody, but not everybody has the wisdom or the guts to play the fool."
>
> Tom Robbins

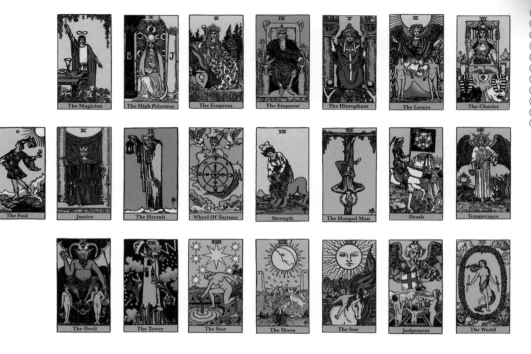

Figure 9: The hero's journey

Lay out the major cards in front of you, as in Figure 9 above. We will uncover The Fool's transformational journey through three phases:

PHASE 1: The making of a hero (cards 1–7)

PHASE 2: Inner alchemy (cards 8–14)

PHASE 3: Enlightenment (cards 15–22)

The Fool starts his adventure with excitement. Leaving his family and all that is familiar behind, he packs all his worldly possessions in a small pouch which he carries on a staff over his shoulder. Is he prepared for the journey? Dressed in colourful clothing, a red feather in his cap symbolising his desires and a garland of flowers over it, he walks carefree under the sun towards his unknown destination. Dreaming about the new opportunities to come, he is about to take a leap off a cliff. His loyal friend, the white dog, is trying to warn him by barking at his feet, but The Fool is not to be deterred.

Phase 1: The making of a hero (cards 1–7)

In the first phase of the journey, we meet the characters that helped shape and prepare The Fool during his childhood and early youth. This is the foundation that prepares him to make his initial decisions and overcome his first conflict.

The Fool meets with The Magician, his mentor – a confident, well-educated young man who teaches The Fool he can bring any idea to realisation in the material when he acts to develop the skills he needs (represented by the four elements on the table in front of him). The Magician's mental abilities, skills and ambitions are symbolised by the clothes he wears: red, representing earthly desires, and white, symbolising purity of spirit and ethical awareness.

Colours are used throughout the tarot to signify various aspects to be developed and integrated. Generally, red represents worldly desires, instincts and power, white symbolises spirit, blue is for intuition, and a purple shawl or veil denotes wisdom. Can you spot these thematic colours in the major cards?

The Fool learns that maintaining balance between the two worlds of spirituality and materialism ensures infinite abundance and success (symbolised by the infinity sign above his head and the snake eating its tail we see wrapped around his waist). Abundance of both worlds is presented by the glorious garden of roses and lilies above The Magician's head and at his feet. We are reminded that gardens have seasons in the same way that all actions will have consequences and yield results in due course. Timing is of the essence to ensure fruition and growth.

Next, The Fool introduces us to the parents who loved and nurtured him. The earthly parents are The Empress and The Emperor. The spiritual parents are The High Priestess and The Hierophant. The Empress represents the gentleness of love, fertility and potential. She is presented sitting on a stone seat on soft, comfortable

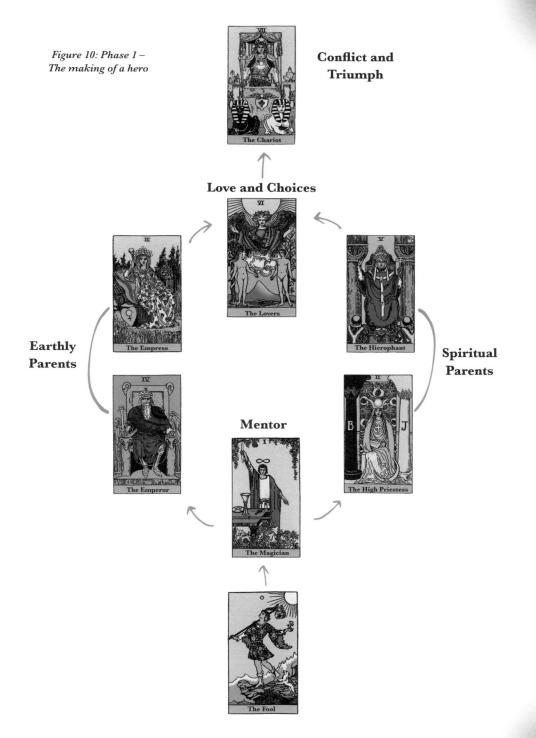

Figure 10: Phase 1 – The making of a hero

Conflict and Triumph

Love and Choices

Earthly Parents

Spiritual Parents

Mentor

cushions. Her dress is draped over her belly, hinting at pregnancy, which symbolises the fertile ground. The 12 stars in her crown symbolise timing: 12 months of the year, the 12 zodiac signs, the 12 hours in a day and 12 hours of night. The nine pearls in her necklace symbolise the nine planets – all hinting at cycles of time: time to plant seeds, to grow and harvest. In front of her is a corn sheath ready to harvest.

Behind The Empress is a luscious green forest and a waterfall in the background symbolises the union of man and woman joining to create new life. It is a scene of calm and abundance. The heart-shaped shield by her feet features the sign of Venus, the ruling planet of Taurus, symbolising nature, love and natural growth. Through his loving mother, The Fool learns about the cycles of birth and death in nature and in relationships between men and women. He can grow to achieve his potential by loving and respecting others as well as nature.

His father, The Emperor, represents the opposite, complementing the qualities of The Empress. He teaches The Fool that inner strength and power is within him, to be wielded appropriately and fairly. He sits on a stone carved throne, looking straight ahead. His red cloak is draped over his armour; the jewelled crown and sceptre symbolise his power and authority over earthly riches. The Fool learns from his father about the importance of discipline to direct his action, ambition and drive. From his two parents, he learns about balance, complementing opposites and that excesses lead to destruction – a common message from other characters The Fool will meet on his tarot journey.

The High Priestess and The Hierophant are the heavenly, or spiritual, parents who help The Fool to integrate his personality, nurture his connection with his inner senses and intuition and urge him to find a higher purpose to his existence. Both spiritual parents complement each other in what they teach The Fool: while The High Priestess represents hidden knowledge of the spiritual world, which the Fool needs patience for in order to gain wisdom, The Hierophant's knowledge and guidance are readily available to support his worldly ambitions.

The Fool's personality is now balanced between earthly and spiritual growth: the feminine, receptive side and the masculine 'doing' and acting; the desire to achieve worldly accomplishments and the wisdom of connecting with a higher spiritual purpose. The integration of opposites enables The Fool to maintain the flow of abundance in his life, while fulfilling his destiny and impacting others' lives. The theme of balance is emphasised repeatedly by the tarot. In this phase, the balance is between the known and the unknown, the hidden and the revealed, the feminine and the masculine, the perceiving and acting. Balance brings wisdom to The Fool. He is a little wiser and ready to make his first decision as a young adult, on his own, when he falls in love.

The Lovers card represents The Fool's first decision-making test. In the picture, the couple stands naked and vulnerable underneath an angel in a beautiful garden. The Fool is facing the woman while she looks up to the angel. It suggests that the 'masculine' intellect needs the emotive, 'passive', feminine input of intuition to help him connect with spirit. In the distance, in between them, we see the destination of the relationship – the mountain top.

The picture suggests that love is complex – it is not what it seems at first! It involves honesty and vulnerability. The Lovers will need to step out of their comfort zone (the garden) and learn to make many decisions together, if the relationship is to reach its heights. The angel is there to help them maintain harmony in their relationship with each other. The Lovers teach The Fool that to come together with another person is a conscious decision and one that can affect his life's journey. A partner with complementing qualities is essential for the success of the journey. The Fool learns to master his thoughts and decisions by collaborating with others and fulfilling his aspirations.

Having overcome his first personal conflict, The Fool is ready to encounter war – or a greater conflict that involves others. The Chariot teaches The Fool that strategic decisions have to be made (symbolised by the star canopy above his head and the star on his crown). Overcoming conflicts requires mastering emotions, as well as clarity of mind. The conflict is presented by the two contrasting black and white lions. First, The Fool must be prepared (as represented by the protection of the armour) and develop the required skills. Then, he must overcome conflicting emotions within him (symbolised by the two lions and the water The Chariot is crossing over). Finally, the effort that needs to be exerted is one of his higher-mind (the stars), namely the ability to see the bigger picture and strategise. Physical strength alone is not enough to secure victory.

Inner Alchemy Integrating Conscious and Subconscious

Figure 11:
Phase 2 – Inner alchemy

Death of Old Self

Stillness, Inner Reflection and Sacrifice

Mastering Inner Desires

Turning Point

Withdrawal and Inner Reflection

Balanced Mind

Phase 2: Inner alchemy (cards 8–14)

The Fool now appreciates the complementary nature of opposing principles and how goals can be achieved by balancing them. The Chariot teaches him to apply mastery over the mind instead of brute force and successfully transcend conflicts.

The next phase of The Fool's development is facing the intricacies of being human, which entails journeying into his inner world to learn about balance, control and higher purpose even further. He has to evaluate the choices he makes and be responsible for their consequences.

Justice teaches The Fool that opposing choices are always present, signified by the sword (the masculine) and by the scales (the feminine). When opposing forces are in harmony, the right choice can be made. Furthermore, choices have consequences because they create change. Justice teaches The Fool that making the right decision involves making a dispassionate choice through the intellect by focusing on facts.

Another lesson Justice teaches is that although circumstance may be dictated, mastering emotions is indispensable to making the right choice. The Justice figure is represented by an androgynous, unbiased character, implying a dispassionate, discriminating intellect. The wisdom of making fair decisions is symbolised by the purple veil behind Justice: balancing opposites requires a balanced mind to achieve harmony – such balance of heart and mind is symbolised by the green and red robes Justice is wearing.

The Hermit enforces The Fool's development by delving deeper into spiritual understanding beyond personal gain. The Hermit is a spiritual mentor and a lone traveller who enlightens the path for others. He teaches The Fool that the bigger decisions in life require a period of solitude, reflection and withdrawal. The Fool has to face his inner fears before he goes any further on his journey. Unlike Justice, who needs to act swiftly and fairly, The Hermit demands patience, implying that wisdom is gained by a clear reflective mind. After a period of solitude, The Fool realises there is more to life than what happens in the busy, distracting, outside world.

He meets next with The Wheel of Fortune, which teaches him about the quick-paced natural cycles of change. Nothing lasts forever: The Wheel of Fortune is a symbol of both stability and change. Therefore, The Fool must be ready to accept and adapt to change, which develops his personal resilience. His period of solitude and reflection quickly changes to a time of moving forward and further development.

Next, The Fool encounters his female spiritual mentor, Strength. The Fool now learns how to discipline and control his inner desires (symbolised by Strength gently taming the lion, who stands for masculine drive). The lesson is: gentleness and controlling instinctive desires is the source of real strength and power. It requires The Fool to integrate his own individuality with endurance and self-control. Now that The Fool's inner and outer resources are in balance, he is ready to move to greater heights by sacrificing his 'old self'. He learns from The Hanged Man that, in order for The Wheel of Fortune to turn in his favour, he must voluntarily give up the old ways of perceiving, thinking and doing.

The Hanged Man represents a period of suspension and delay that is necessary in order to prepare for a new cycle of renewal. By making a conscious choice of letting go of the past, The Fool is able to trust and willing to go through this inner journey into the subconscious. He surrenders childish or false attitudes and habits, as well as beliefs he has outgrown that no longer serve him – and are, in fact, the very cause for this delay. Effectively, he surrenders his ego and any attachment to himself as a 'foolish' immature youngster.

Death confirms the end of the old ways – there is no turning back to the past – and heralds a new beginning. Unless our hero comes to terms with this necessary and permanent change, he will suffer, get stuck and not fully express his potential through a new cycle of growth and maturity.

Temperance represents temporary respite from the ordeals of life. The angel with multi-coloured wings implies divine intervention and hope (the rising sun in the background hints at a future path for The Fool to follow). The angel reminds The Fool that balance and harmony can be achieved throughout the necessary cycles of change as he wakens his subconscious (symbolised by the flowing water between the two cups in the angel's hands) and transforms his evolving self-identity and image. When the flow stops, emotions stagnate and growth is not possible.

Temperance is about regulating emotions to arrive at cooperation, forgiveness and harmony. When dealing with emotions, the need for harmony is further emphasised by the image of the angel standing with one foot on the ground and the other dipping in water, suggesting the need to balance conscious and unconscious emotions to maintain stability and harmony. Where Justice weighs out facts in equal measure, Temperance balances extreme emotions to arrive at a calm and serene state, teaching The Fool how to process feelings of success and failure.

Phase 3: Enlightenment (cards 15–22)

In phase 2, The Fool went through periodic cycles of expansion and limitation that forced him to explore himself further and integrate evolving aspects of his personality. He was also reminded that sometimes, no matter how hard he tries, there will be periods of suspension to prepare him for yet another new cycle of growth. To complete his transformation, he faces similar tests and lessons in phase 3, which are designed to unmask his true self as infinite consciousness in a human body.

The Fool will learn to take a leap to a new level of awareness, while continuing to face his fears and shedding the old ways of perceiving his life and his own image. The final phase is about facing his shadow and dissolving his ego.

Death was the first of a series of dramatic processes of growth, which stripped The Fool of all his worldly pretentions. Now he faces a stern character, The Devil. The picture is strikingly similar to The Lovers, where the couple stand naked, except this time they are chained, in total darkness, by The Devil, symbolising that their imprisonment is by choice. The Lovers can free themselves if they let go of their fears (the chains placed around their necks). They must accept their shadow sides in order to free themselves, otherwise they will remain enslaved by their subconscious fears.

The Tower shakes The Fool's illusions to the ground! Any preconceived values and beliefs about his previous world are shattered to make way for new ones. At last, The Fool leaves the underworld to meet The Star who portends blissful hope and renewal. The young maiden reminds The Fool that to fulfil his purpose – he must stand 'naked', as she does, in truth. He should also remember past lessons (symbolised by the water pool) and use his five senses (presented as the five streams of water pouring from the pitcher in her hand) to awaken his inner senses. The Star signifies rising to new spiritual heights (denoted by the bird perched on the tree behind the maiden) through undergoing emotional experiences. It is our inner guiding star.

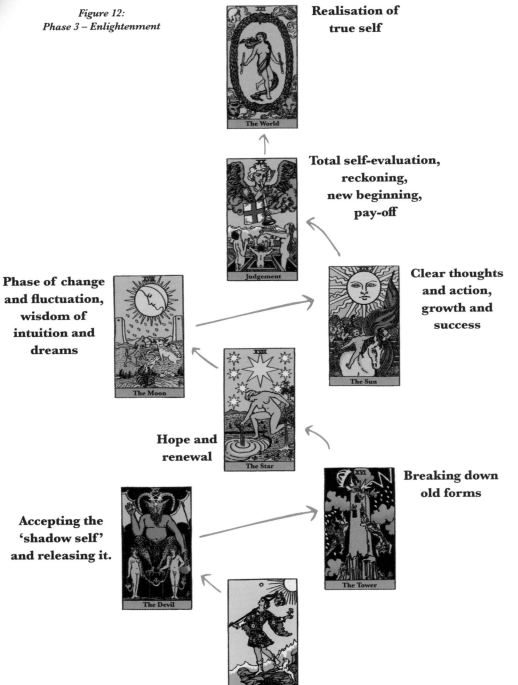

Figure 12:
Phase 3 – Enlightenment

Realisation of
true self

Total self-evaluation,
reckoning,
new beginning,
pay-off

Phase of change
and fluctuation,
wisdom of
intuition and
dreams

Clear thoughts
and action,
growth and
success

Hope and
renewal

Accepting the
'shadow self'
and releasing it.

Breaking down
old forms

In the celestial realm, The Fool next meets with The Moon to address his unconscious and reflect on his mood swings (represented by the various phases of the moon). What makes him emotionally uncomfortable? He finds out that fears embedded in his subconscious will always rise to the surface if not addressed (denoted by the crayfish crawling out of the water). The Moon calls The Fool to integrate the conscious with the subconscious further, symbolised by the presence of two pillars. While The High Priestess, who sits between two pillars with a crescent moon by her feet, signifies the wisdom of the unconscious uncovered in a controlled manner, The Moon indicates that the natural cycles of change have an unpredictable nature. The Fool has to be aware of his fluctuating emotions as he self-transforms: answers to troubling emotions can therefore be found in dreams and through intuition rather than by logic and reason.

After the darkness and the uncertainty of The Moon, The Sun rises above The Fool, signifying clarity of thought, renewed life, fruition and strength. No matter how dark The Fool's journey might get, The Sun will always rise, offering him clear perception and promising success and happiness.

The penultimate experience, however, is Judgement. Now, the angel appears from the clouds calling the dead to rise from the darkness of the subconscious and to stand stripped of their ego and worldly possessions. It is time for The Fool to connect with his higher purpose and to balance all the opposing forces within his personality. Personal progress is now being assessed. The Fool is called to prepare for the resurrection of a new beginning and a new self – his true self. Although the card looks ominous, Judgement in a reading sends a message: 'You have paid your dues; it's a time of rejoicing and renewal.'

The World, which is the last card of The Fool's journey, depicts him floating like a foetus amidst the now – the oval wreath that surrounds him, which contrasts with the small wreath around his hat at the beginning. He is naked – or free from – any false identity or ego-driven personality, and has unified the duality within himself. He has an androgynous appearance, his genitals (symbolising identification with ego) are covered in the purple sash of wisdom. Achieving balance is indicated by the two white wands he carries and the four figures in each corner of the card. Signifying that The Fool understands the natural cycles of change and renewal, the four figures symbolise the four elements and four seasons. The man in the top left corner represents winter/air (personality); the bull in the bottom left signifies spring/earth (desires/fertility); the lion, bottom right, is summer/fire (instincts); and the eagle, top right, is autumn/water (spirit). The Fool, now, is in command of the aspects of his personality, his instincts and desires, and understands his spiritual nature. In a reading, The World signifies the successful completion of a phase of achievement, harmony and fulfilment. The Fool has fully integrated himself and is one with nature and the universe.

From zero to hero

The Fool's journey demonstrates the continuous process of self-development towards achieving enlightenment, over recurring cycles of change. The latter are necessary to induce further growth, integrating the various aspects of being human at each phase. Every time The Fool has to destroy the previous false self to allow the real self to emerge. The journey of self-transformation is demanding. He was forced to reflect inwardly, deepen his awareness and turn to higher wisdom for answers outside himself. Moreover, he was taught to sharpen his thinking and decision-making process, in order to create the best version of himself and to fulfil his hopes and dreams.

The spiritual, or energetic, process of manifesting reality is also revealed. It is a three-fold process, one which is presented several times by the tarot. First, to create a grounding foundation, illustrated by the solid stone thrones on which the characters sit and reign over their domains (The High Priestess, The Empress, The Emperor, The Hierophant, The Chariot and Justice); second, to maintain balance when reacting emotionally to life's events (The Lovers, The Chariot, Temperance, The Devil and Judgement); and, third, to master one's mind, thoughts and instincts (which The Fool learns from The Hierophant, The Chariot, Strength, The Hanged Man, The Star and The Moon).

The Fool's adventure symbolises the innocence of leaving the past behind, and the courage to venture into the unknown future. Through experiencing unexpected losses, The Fool discovers his resolve, and finds a higher purpose – true fulfilment.

INTERPRETATION OF THE MAJOR ARCANA

THE FOOL

The Fool: New beginnings

Signifying sudden opportunities and adventure, The Fool speaks to taking risks, relying on a gut feeling. Unexpected influences. Time to think out of the box. Faith in yourself. Start of an exciting journey – mental, physical or spiritual. Someone who is unconventional.

REVERSED: Recklessness that can lead to disaster. Prepare well before you leap into action.

MODERN INTERPRETATION: Business disrupter. Young entrepreneur. Daredevil.

The Magician: The Initiator

The Magician indicates it is time for action, signifying willpower, sharp intellect, initiative, flexibility, physical/mental travel. Completion of plans. Someone witty, eloquent and at home in the world.

REVERSED: Learning difficulties, confusion, lack of concentration, anxiety, inability to bring ideas to a satisfactory conclusion. Good plans being abandoned.

MODERN INTERPRETATION: Another young entrepreneur. Engineer and designer abilities. Writer. Works in advertising.

The High Priestess: The Unknown

Heightened feminine perceptive nature, secrets to be revealed, the unconscious, guidance through dreams. Developed inner senses. Interest in mystical subjects, psychic abilities. Future unclear at the moment, be patient and wait for the right time.

REVERSED: Negative psychic influences, self-deluded. Overuse of drugs and alcohol. Mental illness, confused mind. Repressed or ignored intuitive feelings. Surrounded by shallow, superficial people. Someone working against you, watch your step, keep your own counsel.

MODERN INTERPRETATION: Highly awakened, sensitive type. Artist, channeller, musician, medium, healer.

The Empress: Abundance

The Empress is about fulfilled potential. Birth, happiness, fulfilment, fertility, pleasure, love affairs, marriage, material gain, creative success, social activity, new project, pregnant woman. Career associated with beauty. Warm, loving, sensual person, loving mother.

REVERSED: Overindulgence. Sterility, miscarriage, end of a love affair, inharmonious influence, unhappy woman. Blocked creativity. Material discomfort. Sex without love, unwanted child, abortion.

MODERN INTERPRETATION: Successful female business owner, art dealer, event organiser, wedding planner, content creator.

The Emperor: Structure

Represents structure, power, wisdom, authority, stability, worldly achievement. Dealing with authority. Prefers to be own boss. Difficulty expressing emotion, unwilling to let defences down.

REVERSED: Immature, selfish, domineering man. Hatred of authority or about to lose power. Feeling threatened, drained, vulnerable, lacking in ambition. Overshadowed by dominant parent.

MODERN INTERPRETATION: CEO, architect, leader, works in armed forces, politician.

The Hierophant: Evolved Mind

Conventional learning. Marriage ceremony. Gifted teacher. Old friend or older person who gives sound advice. High level of consciousness.

REVERSED: Materialistic. Unorthodox. Rebellion against establishment. If seeking advice from accountant or lawyer, take a second opinion. Don't rush into new agreements. Purchases will prove disappointing.

MODERN INTERPRETATION: Lateral thinker. Inspirational speaker, in diplomatic corps, mediator, charismatic actor. Someone with high moral standards.

The Lovers: Partnerships and Love

Love, romance and emotional, spiritual and physical union – soulmate.
Choices are not crystal clear, use your intuition.

REVERSED: Adultery, sex without love, relationship difficulties.
Disrupted sex life. Jealousy. Do not make irrevocable choices at this time.

MODERN INTERPRETATION: Making an important decision that
will affect the rest of your life. Humanitarian activist, support group
leader, specialises in mergers and acquisitions.

The Chariot: Mastery/Transcendence

Hard work is about to be rewarded. Overnight success, material gain. News or friends from long distance. Consistent effort over your struggle is needed. Your inner gifts are about to emerge. Don't delay and get on with it!

REVERSED: Lack of discipline, situation out of control. Addiction, envy, avarice. Afraid to use abilities. Arrogance or lack of self-confidence can be a barrier. Burying head in the sand. Drink and drugs. Warning against overwhelming ambition, burnout, wasting resources.

MODERN INTERPRETATION: Strategist, high-level problem solver, visionary, innovator, specialises in overseas expansion.

Justice: Legal Matters

Favourable settlement of legal matters, signing contracts, karma, justice, negotiations. If making unreasonable demands, you may get less than you hope for. Can indicate choice or decision. Logical.

REVERSED: Complications in legal matters, injustice, imbalance and delays. Major adjustment needed to balance life. Emotional separation.

MODERN INTERPRETATION: Balanced, fair, clear-sighted view of life. Indicates accountants, judges, lawyers, people who make laws.

The Hermit: The Wise Teacher

Withdrawal to initiate higher levels of consciousness. Finding the truth within. Feeling that you have achieved everything you set out to do and wonder what's next. There is always something new to learn. Practise caution and discretion in worldly affairs. Take time to reach conclusions, consider every angle. Experience gained through travel.

REVERSED: Enforced loneliness. Immaturity and superficiality, life full of empty chatter. Don't reject advice given to you. Pig-headedness, refusal to listen. Wasting of time, examine your life and preoccupations. Reconnect with friends.

MODERN INTERPRETATION: Professor, researcher, philosopher, mentor, specialised publisher, historian, experienced therapist, wise intellectual.

Wheel of Fortune: Quick Changes

Strange coincidences, fortunate meetings and lucky breaks shape your life at this time. The wheel has turned and you are beginning a new cycle. Positive confusion reigns. Important not to resist this phase and, when the dust settles, you may find new friends, career or unexpected new home.

REVERSED: Bad luck dogs your path. Be patient, the wheel is always in motion and fate will smile once again. Bad time to initiate new projects or gamble on things going in your favour. Unexpected delays. Change is usually positive at the end. Expect the unexpected.

MODERN INTERPRETATION: Quick changes, external influences which will have great impact.

Strength: The Enchantress

Courage and conviction. Resolute. Grounded, integrated conscious and subconscious. Generous and fair-minded person. Beloved animal could enter your life. In the face of relationship difficulties, open your heart, forgive and forget. Besotted with an older woman. Recovering from illness.

REVERSED: Fear and weaknesses are barriers to success. Your inner strength will help you overcome difficult situations. Success is possible if you overcome fear of failure. Someone who is not in control of their instincts and sexual desires.

MODERN INTERPRETATION: Healing on a deep level. A person who has healing abilities. Animal communication skills. Someone who specialises in conflict resolution. Accomplished personality. Woman of substance and impact. Mentor.

The Hanged Man: Surrender and Sacrifice

Temporary pause in life, inability to move forward. Situation involves others' input and actions. Not right time to make decisions. Will encounter delays. Be patient. Sacrifice old self to grow and reinvent the new.

REVERSED: Warning against selfishness and materialism. Holding on to the past, and failing to grasp new opportunities. Bad investments, loss of belongings and reversals of fortune. Stop and think. Do not let others pressurise you into getting involved.

MODERN INTERPRETATION: Opportunity to reset your life. Will emerge from this period with renewed energy.

Death: Rebirth

Major changes lie ahead, and you may require time to mourn the passing of what you are leaving behind. Loss of some kind, a relationship fails, a friendship ends, a job is lost. Transformation ahead and renewal and start of a new life.

REVERSED: Resisting changes, life very boring. Lethargy and inertia. Stagnation. Unable to adjust to new circumstance.

MODERN INTERPRETATION: Imperative changes that are outside of your control (usually endings) to bring about new beginnings.

Temperance: Harmony Through Balance

Balanced, adaptable influence in life. Can see both sides of the argument clearly. Resolve matters successfully. Calm and in control of events, take whatever fate throws at you. Fresh ideas. Fortunate changes.

REVERSED: Things are out of balance. Quarrels and disagreements. Difficulty in getting on with others. Restless competitiveness. Beware of doing too much, scattering of energy. Poor judgement. Bad health.

MODERN INTERPRETATION: Mediator, motivator, conductor, someone who brings harmony and balance. Making up. Getting together with someone from the past. Promotion at work.

The Devil

The Devil signifies enslavement to obsessions. Overly concerned with material security. Buying friendship or love. Fear, limitations, restrictive circumstances. Delays, difficulties in achieving one's goals. Sexual attraction not love. Destructive, obsessive behaviour. Someone who manipulates and takes advantage, egocentric.

REVERSED: Abuse of power, money, sex, personal charm. Greedy, egocentric, materialistic. Depression. Inability to break from relationship that does not make you happy. Emotional blackmail.

MODERN INTERPRETATION: Emotional and sexual addiction, abusive violent behaviour.

The Tower: Sudden Destruction

Exhilarating change turns your world upside down. Disruptive, even violent. Change is necessary and positive. Break-up of relationships. New lifestyles. Financial losses. Unstable time.

REVERSED: More disruptive and chaotic. Not able to withstand pressure, nervous breakdown. Imprisonment: you will eventually achieve freedom – at a price.

MODERN INTERPRETATION: Sudden awakening or realisation that will change things in your life. Electricity, communication through the internet. Kundalini experience.

The Star: Bliss

Hope, wisdom, adventure, travel, healing, a visionary, imagination, inspiration.

REVERSED: Pessimism, sense of failure. Lost hope, depression, limited vision, doubts.

MODERN INTERPRETATION: Professional sportspeople, and performers who are focused and in control of their minds, people who are telepathic. Divine inspiration. Expansion of personalities and abilities. Telepathic communication (with different worlds).

The Moon: Wisdom of The Unconscious

Psychic impressions, information, dreams. Unexpected change in a situation or feelings. Need for sleep. Rely on self. Mood swings. Emotional changes. Harnessed imagination producing creative output.

REVERSED: Self-deception, self-destruction. Fear of unknown, hallucinations, not seeing problems in true light. Deception from friends. Negative illusions.

MODERN INTERPRETATION: Depression, extreme confusion, emotionally stuck.

The Sun: Joyful Success

Happiness, vitality. Financially better off, enjoying work. Good health. Reaching higher goals where talents and abilities play a great part. A hot country could be significant in terms of fortunate meetings. Successful happy marriage, birth of a child. Rewarding cycle.

REVERSED: Trying harder for success. Vanity and arrogance blocks to success. Difficulties in partnerships, worries about children.

MODERN INTERPRETATION: Any seeds you plant will grow. Masculine principle of healing, achieving material success.

Judgement: Total Transformation

New lease of life, transformation, major decisions, changes, healing has taken place. Spiritual awakening.

REVERSED: Forced changes. Decisions need to be delayed. Stagnation. Delay may lose you something or someone of value. Fear of death/ change. Emotional loss.

MODERN INTERPRETATION: Death of old self. Death of a previous lifestyle.

The World: Total Integration

Achievement and recognition. New cycle of expansion. Sense of completion, accomplishment, success, fulfilment. Time for celebration. New job/promotion. Balanced relationships.

REVERSED: Stagnation, refusal to accept changes Delay in completion, success or achievement.

MODERN INTERPRETATION: Performing on stage, fame, book published, achievements acknowledged by the world. Intelligent wisdom. Further expansion of awareness, self-mastery.

CHAPTER THREE
Tarot numerology

Simply put, the tarot is a series of pictures that tell the story of the experiences we undergo to evolve our understanding of our lives. By extracting wisdom from such experiences, we uncover our true self and fulfil our potential. And, if a picture tells a thousand words, understanding the numbers assigned to each image would probably tell a thousand more! The numbered major cards, in particular, give order to that story (which expands further through the numbered illustrations of the minor cards).

Figure 16 at the end of this chapter, correlates the order of major cards with the number – and the vibration – that identifies them. As you familiarise yourself with the numbers, your interpretation of tarot spreads will improve as your intuition links all the different aspects within the cards together. You will also find additional skills of personal interpretation as your own perspective expands.

> "Numbers are the Universal language offered by the deity to humans as confirmation of the truth."
>
> St Augustine of Hippo – Theologian and philosopher (CE 354–430)

Background of numerology

Numerology is the study of the numerical value of the letters in words, names and ideas. Although, the word 'numerology' was not recorded in the English language before 1907, the philosophers of ancient Greece, such as Pythagoras, Aristotle and Plato, were keen on unlocking the mysteries of our universe by expressing the inter-relationships between various elements and objects in the natural world – the seasons, the planets, sound – and through numbers as early as 500 BCE. They believed that a group of elements shared a certain quality or vibration and could be expressed in a number.

The philosopher Plato, who was a student of Socrates and later taught Aristotle, associated each of the four elements – earth, air, water and fire – with a regular solid shape – cube, octahedron, icosahedron, and tetrahedron, respectively – the so-called Platonic solids. The fifth solid, the dodecahedron, he postulated was aether, the element which made up the heavens. And so, number 4 (The Emperor in the major cards) represents the vibration of stability (the most stable geometric shape is the square), the *builder* (who creates from the four elements of nature) and *space* that manifests in our solid world.

Centuries later, the astronomer Johannes Kepler (1571–1630) revived the idea of using the Platonic solids to explain the geometry of the universe in his first model of the cosmos. By the 18th century the study of sacred geometry, as this exploration of meaningful patterns in the universe became known, was popular with western esotericists. Spiritual knowledge, outside the teachings of the state church, was coded and eventually reflected in the illustrations of the tarot cards – as in the case of the Rider-Waite-Smith tarot deck.

Pythagoras, who is accredited with developing numerology, was a mystic, the first man to call himself a philosopher (a 'lover of wisdom'), and an observer of nature who also believed in the existence of the soul and its journey. When Pythagoras was asked why humans exist, he said, 'to observe the heavens', and it was for the sake of this that he had passed over into life. His theories expressed the relationship through numbers and equations and influenced the work of many, including Aristotle and Plato.

Those who followed his teaching were referred to as Pythagoreans. Among them was St Augustine of Hippo (CE 354–430), a theologian, philosopher and the bishop of Hippo Regius in Numidia, Roman North Africa (now Algeria). His writings on mysticism influenced the development of western philosophy and Christianity. Like Pythagoras, he believed that 'everything had numerical relationships and it was up to the mind to seek and investigate the secrets of these relationships or have them revealed by divine grace'. Aristotle motioned in one of his principal works, *Metaphysics* (350 BCE): 'The so-called Pythagoreans, who were the first to take up mathematics, not only advanced this subject, but saturated with it, they fancied that the principles of mathematics were the principles of all things.'

Pythagoras found correlations between musical notes and numbers, and explained the vibration of string instruments mathematically. It is thought that, from here, the theory that numbers have vibrations was developed. Pythagoreans who followed would take a person's name and date of birth, correlating them to numbers to reveal their outer nature or personality.

On his travels, Pythagoras studied other number systems common at the time, such as the Chaldean number system (the Chaldeans ruled Babylonia from 625 to 539 BCE), regarded as more accurate but more complicated; Zoroastrian philosophy; the Arabic Abjad system, which attributes a numerical value to each letter of the alphabet; the practice in the Jewish tradition of assigning mystical meanings to words based on their numerical value, as well as similar systems using the Latin alphabet and Chinese and Indian numbers. However, it is the Pythagorean number system that seems to have endured in popularity in many cultures and schools of philosophy.

In Pythagorean numerology, specific numbers have mystical properties. The number 1 symbolises unity, the origin of all things (in the tarot it is ascribed to The Magician, see Figure 16 on page 92), since all other numbers are created from it.

The even numbers were regarded as female, the odd numbers male. The number 4 represented justice – the symbol of absolute truth. It stood for the four seasons, the four phases of the moon, stability, structure, space and earth. The most perfect number was 10, because all numbers come from it; it symbolised unity arising from multiplicity. Numbers 11, 22 and 33 were revered as master numbers, and were not reduced to a single digit, because number 1, 2 and 3, respectively, create the Triangle of Enlightenment. The other double digits (44, 55, 66, 77, 88 and 99) were recognised as power numbers, with a special mystical property, because the same number doubled increases its vibration and creates higher potential.

The Pythagoreans recognised the existence of nine heavenly bodies: the Sun, Moon, Mercury, Venus, Earth, Mars, Jupiter, Saturn, and the so-called Central Fire. So important was the number 10 in their view of cosmology that they believed there was a tenth body, Counter-Earth, perpetually hidden from us by the Sun.

A person's date of birth is key to Pythagorean calculations. The Life Path or Birthforce number is the sum of your date of birth reduced to one digit and reflects your personal experiences and the lessons you will learn during your lifetime. For example, if your birthday falls on 25 April 1962, your Life Path number would be calculated in the following way:

Day: 2+5=7, Month: 4, Year: 1 + 9 + 6 + 2) = 18 = 1+8 = 9

Birthforce / Life Path Number: 7+4+9 =11 (Which is a master number.) To arrive at your Life Path number, from the master number 11, add 1+1 which makes 2. This is because Life Path numbers are only from 1 to 9.

Your Birth Day number, which covers your other personality traits, specific abilities and talents that will assist you during your lifetime, is calculated using only the date (without the month or year), reduced to one digit (again, unless it is a master number). So, in the above example, the Birth Day number is 25: 2 + 5 = 7.

Your First Impression number, which relates to the first impression people have of you is calculated by adding the birth day and month numbers only. Again, in the above example, the First Impression number is 2 + 5 + 4 = 11 (again).

Before you read more about the vibrational meaning of numbers, you can already tell that this person has the same number appear twice, number 11 (Strength); and that their Birth Day number is the mystical 7 (The Chariot). So, you might expect a certain quality that is apparent when you first meet them (11), the ability to accomplish goals in their life (11) and to overcome obstacles (7). As we have seen, number 11 is a master number, which is not reduced to a single digit. We will look more closely at the significance of master numbers in the following section.

The vibrational meaning of numbers

In numerology the interconnectedness of all things in the universe is expressed through numbers 1 to 9 only. This is because numbers larger than 9, for example 10, are created by the nine single-digit numbers (1 + 9 = 10).

In modern numerology, however, the number 0 has a special significance, although its value is nought, because its vibration is that of potential on a higher level. So, number 10 has higher potential than 1 – the next octave, if you like. The presence of the zero after a number amplifies and raises its vibration. In personal numerology, the zero amplifies the potential of a life purpose, for example, or highlights innate abilities and calling.

The number of The Fool, the hero of the tarot journey, is zero, which represents the potential to explore a new opportunity ahead. He is about to take a leap and jump off the cliff into the unknown. He is no fool, though! Consider his picture for a moment. He is not an ignorant child, lost as he plays out in the wilderness, who is about to fall. He is a well-dressed young man, who took a decision to leave home, individuate into an independent adult (the next level in his growth) and to form his own understanding of life, taking only the simplest of belongings in the pouch attached to his wand. He is hopeful, looking up to the sky, perhaps unaware of the risk he is taking, though his white dog barks at him to warn him. When you look carefully at the card, you will notice all the potential that zero holds and how The Fool illustration expresses the vibration of a new beginning, with all the rewards and risks that might hold.

Figure 16, later in this chapter (page 92), lists numbers 0 to 9, and the major tarot card that carries the vibration of that number. As such, the vibration of number 1, for example, corresponds to The Magician (1), The Wheel of Fortune (10) and The Sun (19). If you are interested in astrology too, you will also see the corresponding planet that governs that number and the related zodiac sign.

Your numerology profile

The tarot can help you develop a deeper understanding of your vibrational make-up and life purpose when you integrate your knowledge of the tarot with numerology. Completing the walking visualization exercise in Chapter One for the all the major cards will help to deepen the meaning of each step of The Fool's journey and the significance of each card. It will also give you a deeper understanding of the qualities of each card on its own and within a spread.

In this section, you will begin to explore the vibrations and qualities of numbers 0 to 9 and to build your own numerology profile too. In the following section you will integrate both tarot and numerology to build your own tarot profile (page 97).

Your numerology profile is derived from your birthdate. The first step is determining your Birthforce number, which is always a single digit.

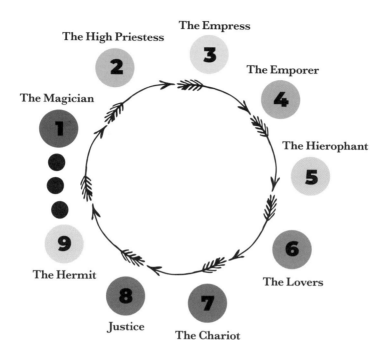

Figure 13: Tarot Birthforce numbers

There is no number that is better than any other. Numbers 1 to 9 express the journey of the soul, or what your consciousness is focused on learning and expressing in this lifetime.

The day of your birth symbolises what you bring forward from your mother's side (represented by the green circle in Figure 14a overleaf) and the year symbolises what you bring forward from your father's side (represented by the red circle). The month symbolises your core essence or main vibration (the blue circle). These three aspects make up your Birthforce number.

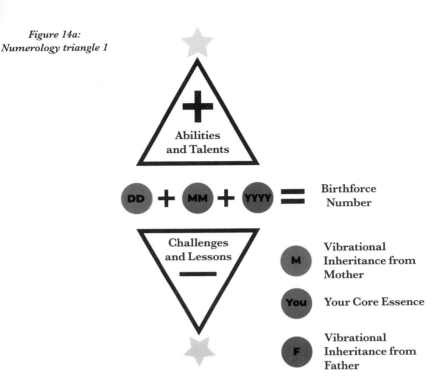

Figure 14a:
Numerology triangle 1

Abilities
and Talents

DD + MM + YYYY = Birthforce Number

Challenges
and Lessons

M — Vibrational Inheritance from Mother

You — Your Core Essence

F — Vibrational Inheritance from Father

The numbers that symbolise your parents' vibrations have nothing to do with how you got on with them. They concern, instead, the abilities, talents and challenges your parents had before you were born – your vibrational inheritance, if you like, which is passed on to you. Any challenges that your parents didn't overcome, or traumas they hadn't healed from, before you were born, will affect your life path vibrationally. For example, if one of your parents had a creative talent in communication, which they didn't express before you were born, that yearning might pass to you.

Vibrational inheritance is an invitation to express that potential in your life. In the same way, the challenges that parents didn't overcome can be seen as an invitation for you to heal them. Your potential talents and abilities, as well as the challenges and lessons you are to learn in this lifetime, are indicated by analysing your birthdate further, see Figures 14b and 14c.

Numerology profile example

Let's say your date of birth is 22 January 1981, this is how you would get your numerology profile: 4 + 1 + 1 = 6.

Your core essence (month number) is 1. Influence through your mother's side is master number 22, which reduces to 4 (2 + 2 = 4). And influence through your father's side is represented by number 1, which is reached by the addition of the single digits of the year (1 + 9 + 8 + 1 = 19 = 1 + 9 = 10 = 1 + 0 = 1). Adding 4 + 1 + 1 = 6 gives you your Birthforce number.

The numbers in the top triangle represent latent abilities and talents and indicate the pinnacle of what you desire to fulfil in this lifetime. To arrive at these numbers, add the single-digit numbers of your birth day and month. Next, add the single digits of your month (mm) to the year (yyyy), represented by the yellow circles in figure 14b. The pinnacle number, your ultimate goal in this lifetime, is reached by adding the two numbers you just calculated together.

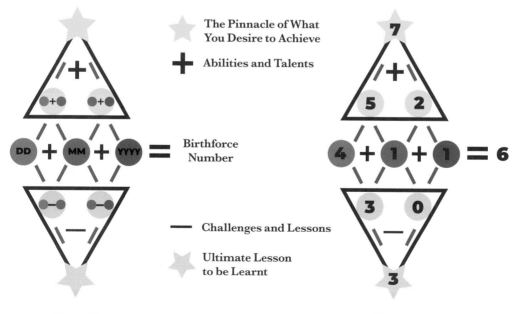

Figure 14b:
Numerology triangle 2

Figure 14c:
Numerology triangle 3

In Figure 14c, you can see the numbers in the bottom level of the top triangle become: 2 + 2 + 1 (or 4 + 1) = 5 and 1+1 = 2, respectively. Adding these two numbers together gives you the pinnacle number, which in this case is 7 (5 + 2 = 7).

Similarly, you reach the numbers in the bottom triangle by subtracting the same birthdate numbers from each other (instead of adding them). So, your challenges are 4 - 1 = 3, and 1 - 1 = 0, and the ultimate challenge is 3 - 0 = 3, see Figure 14c.

You can also calculate your Personal Year, which represents underlying influences in the current year activated as of your birthday in that year. In order to do this, add your birth day (dd) and birth month (mm) to the current year. In this example your Personal Year would be 5 + 2022 = 5 + 6 = 11. The following section delves deeper the numerology of number 1 to 9, the influence number 0 has and how it relates to the numbers of the major cards.

Numerology of the major arcana

NUMBER 0: New Beginning (The Fool)

Without zero, the numbers that follow nine would not exist! Although zero has no value, vibrationally, it holds the potential of all that is to come. The Fool starts his journey with the innocence of a child, lacking the logic of a mature person, and is therefore unaware of the risks that a new beginning may pose. Yet, if he does not take action, he will not find out. Zero reminds us that there is potential for success or failure, if one is not careful, but action must be taken. When zero appears with another number, it heightens the potentiality of that number and amplifies its vibration.

NUMBER 1: Inner Resources and Unity (The Magician)

Number 1 has the potential within it to create all other numbers. It has the vibration of taking initiative, leadership and powerful mental creativity to express its unique identity. Like The Magician, number 1 has all the elements required within his reach to manifest his dreams successfully. However, balance must be maintained throughout for dreams and ideas to come to fruition successfully.

The Magician represents this balance as he raises one arm to the heavens, holding a white wand that represents purity (of intention and spiritual awareness). He points one finger down at the earth with the other hand, representing logic, practicality and earthly skills. Number 1, like The Magician, transforms potential into reality through, skill, dexterity, logic, discipline and flexibility. The infinity sign above The Magician's head indicates: 'If you stick to this formula, you can create infinite possibilities.'

POSITIVE: Inspiration for others, original, dynamic, self-determined.

NEGATIVE: Domineering, intolerant, impulsive, aggressive, egotistic, proud.

NUMBER 2: Duality and heightened sensitivity (The High Priestess)

Known as the diplomat, or the peacemaker, number 2 carries the vibration of a higher sense of perception and gentleness. Like The High Priestess, it has the ability to perceive the wants and needs of others as well its own (which makes an excellent counsellor). Number 2 represents duality because it can see both sides of the coin, itself and the other, and has an inner sense of logic, as well as imagination. It is aware of its spiritual principles, as well as the logical means to materialise things physically.

Number 2 perceives the visible as well as the unseen and right from wrong. It expresses the vibration of psychic potential (perceiving communication from spirit, dreams or animals), and receiving messages from the subconscious through dreams. It therefore bridges the two worlds, spiritual and physical, or conscious and unconscious. Number 2 has to learn how to balance itself, otherwise its sensitivity will overwhelm it: like a sponge, it can absorb any kind of water (a symbol of emotions). It has to learn to trust its abilities, become independent and choose its surrounding atmosphere carefully.

POSITIVE: Gentle, sincere, psychic, feminine qualities.

NEGATIVE: Too adaptable, moody, timid.

NUMBER 3: Joy and Creativity (The Empress)

Number 3 is the fruitful result of 1 + 2, the initiator (number 1) and the perceiver (number 2), which equals abundant joy and success of self-expression. It contains the vibration of giving, a deep aesthetic sense and understanding of the creative arts, and practical common sense as well as inspiration. Its joyfulness makes it a pleasure to be with.

Like The Empress, number 3 has an inner urge to create, to give birth (figuratively and physically) and to communicate, making it a natural speaker and lending itself well to careers such as marketing and PR. As a creator, not a labourer, it has the power to make the impossible possible, though it needs the help – or input – of other numbers to put its creative imagination into form.

POSITIVE: Artistic, gifted with words, joy-bringer.

NEGATIVE: Restless, over-worrying, emotional nervous tension.

NUMBER 4: Stability (The Emperor)

Number 4, The Emperor, signifies the laying down of law and order. It is the vibration of the builder, grounded ability, fairness, order and discipline, but is focused on results. It is organised and creates methodology, routine, rhythm and process, because it values time, meeting deadlines and achieving results. The structures it builds are long-lasting and stable. When overdisciplined, it can be obstinate, inflexible, or micromanage details, instead of focusing on the big picture.

The vibration of number 4 values space and time, therefore its environment has to be in order, and routine must be established it order for it to build a stable throne, or legacy, that lasts. All things have to be seen right to the end. People with number 4 as their Birthforce number have very special work to accomplish in their lifetime. Their energies and ideas have to be well grounded to maintain them while they change their environment. Number 4 is the vibration of the order in nature, and it contains all the elements within it. It makes for very practical people with self-discipline and perseverance.

POSITIVE: True builder, seriousness, disciplined.

NEGATIVE: Obstinate, fixed opinion, lacks imagination.

NUMBER 5: Freedom (The Hierophant)

The structures that The Emperor builds, utilising vibrations of all the preceding numbers, brings freedom of expression on a higher level. Number 5, the rolling stone, represents changes, adventure, freedom of thought and freedom in action. Like a rolling stone, it leads to something new (and not necessarily something stable). It is agile, adaptable and versatile – ready to grab the nearest opportunity quickly. It is a strong vibration of all that is new and needs a great deal of freedom to materialise it. Number 5 understands the law of change, or destiny, the restless inner nature and the love of travel and exploration, because it brings about new experiences and understanding that helps it to evolve.

Like The Hierophant, it is well-connected with its inner senses, as well as with its higher purpose or consciousness, which gives it great resourcefulness. People influenced by number 5 may not be aware of what they know until they are prompted. They have the ability to sense other people's lives, embody their point of view and teach others about 'freedom'. The downside is that their freedom-loving nature might distract them from coming back to their own lives. They can easily get bored if not stimulated. Their challenge is maintaining the balance between the desire to explore and staying focused on their own life path.

POSITIVE: Great communicator, great attraction to the opposite sex, quick-thinking, curious.

NEGATIVE: A rolling stone, ill-tempered, restless, nervous.

NUMBER 6: Personal Love, Peace and Harmony (The Lovers)

People who have number 6 as their Birthforce number have a need for harmony, truth, fairness and an obligation to bring all this to their environment. Number 6, The Lovers, has the vibration of personal love. Such people balance themselves by coming together with others who share their needs and values. Number 6 loves by nurturing, giving and creating harmonious communities and families. It needs a goal for its devotion for happiness can only be experienced if these gifts are used in service for others.

It grows and heals by learning the lessons of how much to give, and what not to give, through personal relationships. Number 6 has a great love for children and is therefore a very good teacher. The challenge of number 6 is not to make others emotionally dependent on it, or to become overprotective and possessive. It must therefore be mindful of its intentions and motives to remain in balance.

POSITIVE: Harmony, service, love of home life.

NEGATIVE: Jealous, whinges, falls for flattery, stubborn.

NUMBER 7: Mastery (The Chariot)

Number 7 is the visionary mystic, who masters inner and outer senses and resources. Like The Chariot, it is spiritual but not religious, an independent thinker and formulator of mindful strategy. By reflecting on its experiences and honing its skills, it is determined to conquer its dreams successfully. As children, people with number 7 as their Birthforce number are naturally intelligent, inquisitive and seek a deeper meaning behind all things. They may seem shy or introverted, as they contemplate the world around them.

Solitude is required for self-analysis and deep thinking and exploring number 7's inner mystical and philosophical nature; their gifts may not be immediately obvious to others. Number 7 is the vibration of soul growth. Only in silent exploration will the answer to life's problems arise from within. Number 7 has a strong sense of self-control and a tendency to repress emotions as it builds a protective wall around itself. However, once it is well-acquainted with its inner gifts and surroundings, it overcomes its fear of 'stepping outside' and its charm is revealed. Such people, given their ability to control their minds and make great effort seem effortless, often excel at sports.

POSITIVE: Inspired, wise, loves solitude, charming.

NEGATIVE: Deluded, in danger of drug addiction, repression issues, cynical, lacks generosity, doesn't put in the effort.

NUMBER 8: Delicate Balance (Justice)

Number 8 is the most misunderstood of all numbers in numerology! It is often associated with money, success and fame, but its real power lies in the delicate balance which it must maintain – otherwise things can fail just as dramatically as they can succeed. It is the vibration of Justice and righteousness, balancing spirituality and materialism – so be careful what you wish for, or you might tip the scales and suffer cycles of huge gain and loss. Number 8 teaches the importance of evolution on all three levels – physical, emotional and mental – to manifest harmoniously. It represents karma in the sense of 'as above, so below'. Often, number 8 does not recognise its power, so it endures long periods of waiting and the mental frustration of repeated attempts before it expresses its greatness.

To maintain its achievements, number 8 needs a higher purpose for its success to benefit humanity rather than act from the ego or greed alone. It is a strong and quick-acting vibration with tangible results. A small step in the right direction will bring success, and the opposite is also true. Life can be a constant cycle of dramatic endings and rebirths, giving you the opportunity to learn, and transmute your challenges into victories. Don't give up on your dreams. Number 8 is an opportunity to reinvent and evolve; intentions and actions must therefore be aligned with the heart and not the ego.

POSITIVE: Energetic, realistic, capable, strong, authoritative.

NEGATIVE: Overly money-minded, struggles with expressing emotions, forceful and can be impatient.

NUMBER 9: Fulfilment and Completion (The Hermit)

Number 9 is the final number and has the vibration of completion. Within it, all numbers are contained. There is no limit to its promise, but responsibility has to be accepted. It represents the wise teacher, or The Hermit, who went into solitude to learn about himself and find a higher purpose to life. It is the number of experience, inner knowledge, intellect and compassion for humanity.

People whose Birthforce number is 9 can suffer greatly for others until they learn that it doesn't help, while the right action without prejudice can. It is also the highest form of love – one which does not bind but can detach, stand back and remain deeply concerned. Your life path is asking you to see a project through to completion, observe the wider picture and believe in your own greatness. Your greatest challenge is detachment, objectivity and compassion, when acting from your heart, you will touch all those around you.

POSITIVE: Idealistic, forgiving, humanitarian, charitable.

NEGATIVE: Possessive, selfish, narrow-minded, susceptible to mood swings and bouts of depression.

MASTER NUMBERS: 11, 22 and 33

The master numbers (11, 22 and 33 only) are often not reduced to one digit, because they have a higher vibration, or more potential, than all the other numbers. Moreover, because numbers 1, 2, 3 create all other numbers and possibilities, other double digits (44, 55 and so on) are referred to as power numbers, but don't carry the intense vibration of the master numbers. If your Birthforce number is a master number, you might feel you are meant to do something special.

However, such people can be intense and difficult to handle, because they demand balance of motive and intention, the spiritual and the materialistic, and are activated by greater understanding and awareness. They operate for the good of humanity, and from the heart and higher mind rather than personal ego. Nonetheless, their vibration is an invitation for you to aim higher, and expand your perspective and imagination.

NUMBER 11: The Gateway To Enlightenment

This number carries double the potential of number 1 and its vibration is amplified further since 11 is 10 + 1. It contains all the numbers within it, and therefore is an octave higher, if you like, of number 1. When 11 is reduced to 2, it carries the vibration of that number as well. Therefore, number 11 includes natural intelligence (1) and increased sensitivity, spiritual insight and higher intuition (2). It is seen as the gateway to enlightenment.

Let's compare The High Priestess (2) and Strength (11). Although The High Priestess is perceptive and intuitive, she sits between two pillars of duality, with a veil behind her, representing more truth to be uncovered. Unlike Strength, whose acceptance of her intuitive abilities has led to greater understanding of spiritual truths – which she is always connected to (represented by the infinity sign above her head). Strength has become a master, channelling this understanding into healing. She has tamed and harnessed

Figure 15: Comparing the numerology of The High Priestess and Strength

instinctive 'wild' desires within, which have transmuted into a charmed harmonious reality. Number 11 symbolises the potential to push the limitations of human experiences, our ability for diplomacy and integrating these endeavours in the highest spiritual understanding. It bridges the polarity between being human and consciousness, ignorance and enlightenment, on the precipice of which The High Priestess sits. It is a number that represents ultimate power or strength.

NUMBER 22: Grand Success Through Mastery

The next master number, 22, is 11 doubled and it has many of the insights of number 11, Strength, combined with methodology and practicality, represented by number 4 (2 + 2 = 4). Number 22 manifests its potential physically in a disciplined, practical and methodical manner with the confidence and leadership of number 4 (The Emperor), and the spiritual mastery of number 11 (Strength). It represents the ultimate effortless manifestation of ideas into reality, or spiritual understanding into the material world.

Figure 16: Numerology of numbers 1 to 9 and corresponding major cards

NUMBER	KEYWORD	CORRESPONDING PRIMARY VIBRATION	VIBRATIONAL QUALITIES
0	New beginning	The Fool	Anything is possible, taking a risk into the unknown
1	Inner resources, unity	The Magician	Initiative, leadership
			-
2	Duality, heightened sensitivity	The High Priestess	Balancing, subtlety, hidden matters, clairvoyance
			Karmic transition
3	Joy, creativity	The Empress	Abundance, fertility, creativity.
			Expanded abundance

NUMBER 33: Evolved Consciousness

Number 33 is considered to represent the master teacher. It is the most influential number as it contains within it the potential of preceding master numbers 11 and 22. Instead of focusing on personal ambitions (qualities of the abundant 3, The Empress), it focuses its abilities on empowering humanity with sincere devotion on a higher octave ($3 + 3 = 6$ = The Lovers, the card which relates to service to others). Figure 16 summarises the vibrational qualities of numbers 0 to 33 and their expression in the tarot. Together, the tarot and numerology symbolise the personal development of an individual in a lifetime. You can use this table as reference to complete your personal tarot profile.

SECONDARY VIBRATIONAL REPRESENTATIONS	CORRESPONDING GOVERNING PLANET	ZODIAC SIGN
-	-	-
10 Wheel of Fortune ($1 + 0 = 1$) 19 The Sun ($1 + 9 = 10 = 1$)	Sun	Leo
11 Strength ($1 + 1 = 2$) 20 Judgement ($2 + 0 = 20 = 2$)	Moon	Cancer
12 The Hanged Man ($1 + 2 = 3$) 21 The World ($2 + 1 = 3$)	Jupiter	Sagittarius

4	Stability	The Emperor	Structure, rhythm, time and space
5	Freedom	The Hierophant	Changes, adaptability, curiosity
6	Personal love, peace, harmony	The Lovers	Love, service to others though partnerships, harmony
7	Mastery	The Chariot	Transcendence, balance, growth, spirituality
8	Delicate balance	Justice	Fine balance, justice, fairness
9	Fulfilment completion	The Hermit	Anything is possible, taking a risk into the unknown
11	The gateway to enlightenment	Strength	Mastering instinctive desires to create reality
22	Grand mastery		Master builder
33	Evolved consciousness		Impacting humanity

13 Death (1 + 3 = 4)	Uranus	Aquarius
14 Temperance (1 + 4 = 5)	Mercury	Gemini
15 The Devil (1 + 5 = 6)	Venus	Taurus
16 The Tower (1 + 6 = 7)	Neptune	Pisces
17 The Star (1 + 7 = 8)	Saturn	Capricorn
18 The Moon (1 + 8 = 9)	Mars	Aries

1 The Magician
2 The High Priestess

2 The High Priestess
4 The Emperor

3 The Empress
6 The Lovers

YOUR BIRTHDAY: DD/MM/YYYY (E.G. 22/1/1981) X + X + X (4+1+1)	NUMBER	TAROT CARD (S) REPRESENTATION
Your Core Essence (month)	1	The Magician
Influences from mother's side (birthday)	22/4 = 4	The Emperor Master Number 22
Influences from father's side (birth year)	19/10 = 1	The Sun, Wheel of Fortune, The Magician
Birthforce/Lifepath number (addition of birthdate digits)	6	The Lovers
Hidden Talent and Abilities (numbers in the top triangle by adding DD + MM, and MM + YYYY respectively)	5 and 2	The Hierophant and The High Priestess
Ultimate Goal/Pinnacle (addition of Hidden Talent and Abilities numbers)	7	The Chariot
Challenges To Overcome and Lessons To Learn (subtraction of DD - MM, and MM - YYYY respectively)	3 and 0	The Empress and The Fool
Ultimate Challenge To Overcome or Lesson To Learn (subtracting numbers of challenges and lessons)	3	The Empress
Personal Year (if current year is 2022) (addition of DD + MM to current YYYY)	11	Strength

Figure 17: Your personal tarot profile

Your personal tarot profile

Building your personal tarot profile brings your understanding of both tarot and numerology together in a practical way, presenting your birthdate numbers through the corresponding tarot cards. Your personal profile gives you further insights into your own make-up, what you hope to achieve and overcome in this lifetime.

Considering the previous birthdate example, 22 January 1981, (22/4 +1 + 10/1) makes a Birthforce or Life Path number of 6.

When considering birthdate numbers, it is worth noting down additions higher than 9, since they are represented in the major tarot cards numbered 1 to 21. These provide additional insights into the underlying influences within your birthdate. Also, make a note of any additions that result in any of the master numbers (11, 22, 33) as they reflect further expansion and higher potential.

In our example, the birth day is 22, which is a master number. It is reduced further into 4 (2 + 2 = 4). The birth month is January which equals 1, and the birth year = 1 + 9 + 8 + 1= 19 reduces to 1 (1 + 9 = 10 = 1). The zero here amplifies the vibration of number 1 and is expressed as 10/1, or 10 into 1.

22 . 1 . 1981

$\downarrow$

22/4 . 1 . 19/10

$\downarrow$

22/ 4 . 1 . 1 19/10/

$\downarrow$

7

5 + 2

4 + 1 + 1 = 6

3 - 0

3

secondary
underlying
influences

*Figure 18:
Numerology and
tarot example*

Now, let's look at the insights we gain by combining numerology with the corresponding tarot cards.

Insights from numerology

* This person's core essence is 1, which holds the potential of all other numbers.

* What they bring forward from their mother's side is the ability to build a lasting legacy by discipline and methodology. They have the potential to expand this further, impacting humanity.

* What they bring forward from their father's side is the potential for huge success once they hone their abilities; integrating intuition and logic, they will realise their dreams (10 amplified).

* What they are building up to is mastering the laws of manifestation, spirit and matter, overcoming all obstacles (7).

* Their challenge is accepting all this potential within, 3, and to connect and communicate with the right people who can support and help them grow. They need to believe in their own ability to succeed while staying connected to who they are.

* Their Birthforce number, 6, tells us that they can be of service to humanity. Honing their abilities and overcoming their challenges will lead them to finding peace, love and harmony through the right partnerships (romantic and business).

* This year's underlying influence is 11 (5 + 2022 = 11) signifying the possibility of greater spiritual understanding and taking a leap (master number 11) to operate on a higher level of mastery. What they achieve will impact and inspire others.

Insights from corresponding tarot cards

* This person's date of birth reveals the innate ability to integrate logic and intuition (The Magician) which is emphasised three times in their numbers.

* What they bring from their mother's side is the ability to combine their

structure and logic (The Emperor) with intuition (The High Priestess expressed as 22 into 4). They have a strong psychic disposition to perceive what others usually can't (The High Priestess).

* They have a deep spiritual side and are quite evolved (5 and 2; The Hierophant and The High Priestess, respectively); they are ethical and perceptive and destined for great accomplishments.

* From their father's side, they have the ability to move forward quickly (10, The Wheel of Fortune) once they understand that they need to find balance between their dreams and working towards them (The Magician). They can achieve huge success (19, The Sun) benefiting all those around them.

* Their challenges reveal that the communication is key. They can nurture others around them and achieve materialistic abundance (3, The Empress), providing that they are cautious about taking risks (0, The Fool), particularly concerning who they invite in their lives (3, The Empress).

* This year, they have the opportunity to grow profoundly (11, Strength) by mastering their desires and impulses, and grounding their intentions. What they can achieve is infinite!

Take a few moments to consider Figure 16. Look at the patterns of the numbers and the major cards. What else do the numbers and tarot tell you?

....

....

....

CHAPTER FOUR
Reading the cards

The tarot is a combination of pictures and numbers that tell the story of The Fool's self-development. He is about to take a risk, stepping out of his comfort-zone and embarking on a journey on his own to find out who he is. Using the tarot cards facilitates a creative process of imagination that helps you to think outside the box and seek inspiration and guidance – at whatever stage you are in your life's journey.

When you formulate your question and pick out the cards for a spread, the magic of the tarot comes into play! A tarot reading is interpreting the story told through the cards according to the context of the question and the layout sequence of the cards. Give yourself a few moments to look at the pictures, travel into each card, consider its vibrational number and then ask yourself: 'What story do the tarot cards reveal?' Your intuition will be ready to answer.

> *"I ask for guidance from the Highest Source*
> *for the highest good of all concerned.*
> *I ask that 'jokers' be banned from this experience.*
> *I ask that guidance is crystal clear,*
> *that I remain protected at all dimensions of time-space,*
> *I ask that I remain grounded, and*
> *that I am replenished*
> *when I am done.*
> *And so it is."*
>
> *Invocation for consulting tarot cards*

Methodology

To start with, you might want to begin with a short invocation, or a prayer, setting your intention. Formulating your question clearly and writing it down will help you decide on the appropriate spread to answer that question. For example, is it a short-term issue or a long-term one? Pick up your major cards and shuffle them in one direction to clear their energy. Then, continue shuffling while focusing on your question. Repeat it in your mind as you shuffle. Whenever you feel like it, reverse a total of two major arcana cards at random.

When you feel you are ready to receive guidance, put the cards face down on the surface in front of you. Spread them out in a line, then pick a number of them randomly, without thinking too much, according to your chosen spread. To receive unbiased guidance, detach your emotions from the outcome. Feeling the cards, for example, and then picking them out would be a mistake. You could be feeling the energy of the card itself, rather than being guided to select the appropriate one. Before you ask another question, shuffle the cards to clear them, and then repeat the process: shuffling the cards while you ask your question in your mind and reversing two major arcana cards at any time before you put the cards down.

The following points might help you remember the reading sequence:

* Identify what you wish for guidance on.

* Is it short-term or long-term?

* Phrase the question in the right way.

* Decide on a spread.

* Separate major and minor cards.

* Clear the cards by shuffling in one direction.

* Focus on one question.

* Reverse two major arcana cards.

* Spread the cards in front of you.

* Randomly pick cards (don't think too much!)

* Lay the cards down according to the sequence of your chosen reading template.

How to phrase a question / choose a tarot spread

Phrasing the question around the issue you wish for guidance on will clarify your mind and guide you to the relevant spread to choose. Keep it simple! What's your story? What's your issue? Write down a brief description.

Your answer might be of a general nature or you might want to highlight the theme for the next phase of your life. For example, 'Today is an important one for me – how will it go?' Or 'Today is my birthday – what is my new year about?' Choosing the one-card spread in these instances will undoubtedly identify the theme for you. At other times, you might be about to decide on a specific concern. For example, your answer might be: 'I am looking for a property. I saw two options – which one is right for me?' The strategy would be to ask two separate questions, one for each property. Asking if option A or B is better for you will not yield a clear answer. A better way of phrasing a question around this topic would be: 'Is this the right time to invest in buying a property?' Then to ask: 'What about buying property A?' That would be followed by: 'What about buying property B?' In this way, you will receive more guidance around the question, compare the answers and get your advice. Since this is an immediate short-term decision, either the three-card or yes-or-no spread would be appropriate.

When your issue is a specific one concerning something that is currently happening in your life, where the answer is either 'Yes, go ahead' or 'No, this will not happen', the yes-or-no spread will give you answers right away. An example might be: 'Will I succeed in securing this contract?' Or 'What about accepting Joe Bloggs's marriage proposal?'

Phrasing the question in such a way − 'What about so and so issue?' − helps you to stay objective when interpreting the answers. It can also clarify or identify factors and other influences around this issue. For example, if you are at the outset of a relationship, or a project, asking 'What about my relationship with Joe Bloggs?' or 'What about project X that I am involved in right now?' will yield underlying factors or issues that need to be considered, which will guide you to a better outcome. Guidance can come in the form of deeper insights around the reasons why you attracted such an experience, or the lessons that you need to learn from it. In this case, when your intention is to uncover and clarify influences you may not be aware of, choosing the five-card Star spread will shed light on those issues and give you the outcome.

Additionally, when you are emotionally invested in an issue such as relationship or physical health, you might discover that you are unable to get clear answers. This is normal. Instead, try to phrase the question as if you are asking it about another person who has the same name. For example, if your name is John, and you are asking about your relationship with X, your question would phrased as follows: 'What about John's relationship with X?' Asking in this way will distance you from the outcome, and the cards might just give you the advice you seek.

At other times, you may wish for guidance on the big picture or your long-term future, with details to guide you on the way. For example, at New Year or on birthdays or when doing a comprehensive reading for a friend. In these cases, try the 12-house astrological spread, which is ideal for annual guidance. It is slightly more complex than other spreads. Usually, you would phrase the question along these lines: 'What will be the important changes in my life?' Or 'What do I need to know about the next 12 months?' We will look more closely at tarot spreads and sample readings later on in this chapter.

Questions you can ask

Now that you have an overview of how to phrase a question and how to choose the right spread, here are a few suggestions of topics you can seek guidance on, using any of the short-term spreads. Keep a record of your spreads, because time will reveal more information to you.

* What do I need to know about… (today, this week, this month, this project, dealing with this person)?

* What about the way I feel now?

* What about the issue I have in mind?

* What does my heart tell me?

* What is holding me back?

* What are my strengths or weaknesses?

* Why am I experiencing this obstacle?

* What will help me overcome this situation?

* What is my relationship with … about?

* What can I learn from this experience?

* What about the idea I have in mind for a business?

* What is my dream about?

* What is this (person) teaching me?

* What is the best way to handle this issue?

* What do I need to focus my energies on?

* What can help me attract the right soulmate for this lifetime?

* What field is the right area of business for me to pursue at this point in my life?

* What about my physical health? What about the physical health of X?

Frankly, you can ask for guidance on any subject in any area of your life, including your pets, providing you phrase your questions clearly and keep an open mind to receiving the answer. Sometimes, we might not like the guidance we receive, or it might not be what we hoped for. Asking about the same topic over and again, especially when we are emotionally entangled, will not give a clearer answer. In fact, you might end up more confused, or interpret the cards as saying what you would like them to. What you can do, if answers are not clear, is to put the cards away, take a break, and try asking another time when you are in a calmer state of mind and therefore more objective.

Interpreting answers

Whether you are using a short-term spread, or a long-term one, sometimes the end card, or the result card, needs to be followed in order to clarify the outcome even further. For example, your result card might be The Fool, in which case it is telling you that you are about to take a leap, start in a new direction, or take an unknown risk. However, you still do not know how this new direction will turn out, or whether taking that leap or risk would be fruitful. In this instance, you would pick one more card to see if you get a definitive answer. Another example is when the Wheel of Fortune is an outcome card. It denotes unexpected quick changes in your situation, so, you follow it with another card to see the nature or outcome of those changes.

Each tarot card has a slightly different meaning when it appears reversed in a reading, as opposed to its meaning when it appears upright. Generally, if you tune into the illustration of the card, or try the 'walk into the picture' visualisation on page 34, you will intuit its reversed meaning. When a reversed card appears in a spread, it is highlighting underlying factors you need to become aware of. The table below summarises the meaning of each of the major cards when they appear as the end or the result card in a spread.

	CARDS	ANSWER WHEN CARD IS UPRIGHT	CARDS TO FOLLOW	ANSWER WHEN CARD IS REVERSED
0	The Fool	YES (But follow with another card to see the quality of the outcome)	✓	NO. Bad risk and a serious mistake
1	The Magician	YES	-	NO. Lack of communication or abilities
2	The High Priestess	All information is not in place (Follow with another card)	✓	NO
3	The Empress	YES	-	NO, will not do well
4	The Emperor	YES (But with a lot of effort)	-	NO, stressful
5	The Hierophant	YES, destined for it	-	YES, needs unconventional approach
6	The Lovers	Important decision (Follow with another card)	✓	NO, partnership will fail

7	The Chariot	YES, brilliant!	-	NO, don't force it - let it go
8	Justice	YES (Follow to see the quality of the outcome)	✓	NO, contract will be broken, or will not happen
9	The Hermit	Not now (Follow with another card)	✓	NO, confused
10	Wheel Of Fortune	Quick changes (Follow with another card)	✓	No decision
11	Strength	YES	-	NO, no initiative, inner resources or good will
12	The Hanged Man	There is delay, suspended	✓	Delayed (Follow with another card)
13	Death	Won't happen, no answer (But follow with another card)	✓	NO
14	Temperance	YES	-	NO, matters are out of balance
15	The Devil	NO (But follow with another card)	✓	NO (But follow with another card)
16	The Tower	No answer – everything is changing (Follow with another card)	✓	NO (Follow with another card)
17	The Star	YES	-	Will happen, but may be delayed

18	The Moon	You are in doubt at the time of the reading (Follow with another card)	✓	You are not getting what you want (Follow with another card)
19	The Sun	YES		YES, but it could be a compromise (Follow with another card)
21	Judgement	No decision is made yet at time of reading, ask again another time	✓	NO, judgement is against you
21	The World	YES, expansion	-	NO

Figure 19: Result cards and whether to follow in a spread

Tarot card spreads and sample readings

The One-Card Spread

A one-card spread is ideal to use when your intention is to identify a theme or focus to an upcoming period or experience. The best way to phrase a question would be: 'What do I need to know about... (today, this week, this month, this project, experience I am going through, or person I am dealing with)?' Or simply, 'What about the issue I have in mind?'

SAMPLE READING: Nadine, who is single and in her early thirties, wonders about why she has not yet met the right person, when other areas of life are going well.

QUESTION: 'What does Nadine need to know about meeting the right person in her life?'

CARD(S): Judgement. Followed by The Hierophant.

INTERPRETATION: Nadine is going through a significant personal transformation. This 'waiting' period is intentional to allow her to reinvent her unique life and self. She needs the space and time to focus on her own growth to allow the new self to emerge and form. Becoming aware of the choices she makes on a daily basis would help her to align with her life purpose.

The Hierophant tells us that she is destined to go through this transformation, which will lead to a deeper awareness and sense of knowing and align her with her destiny. However, she will meet the person she is destined to be with at the right time, after forging her own way, identity and reality. There is no indication of timing, because the outcome will transpire once her transformation is complete.

The Three-Card Spread

The three-card spread is a versatile template. It provides a quick overview of a situation using the major cards only. With experience and practice, you can add the minor cards later on, placing one above each major card.

Follow the same methodology detailed earlier (page 101) of reversing two major cards. Pick three cards laying them in the order indicated in Figure 21. The first card represents the past, the second signifies the present and any action needed, and the final card concerns a future outcome. In the table overleaf, Figure 20, I've suggested other examples of a three-card spread. For example, the first card can represent the subconscious, the second the conscious, and the final card higher wisdom. Can you come up with other variations? Add them to the table and try them!

SAMPLE READING: Nick, in his late forties, suffered numerous setbacks due circumstances outside his control. He has finally found his life's passion in personal fitness training and wants to check it is the right career path for him.

QUESTION: 'What about Nick's newly found vocation?'

CARDS IN THE SPREAD: 1 – The World, 2 – The Hanged Man, 3 – The Empress

INTERPRETATION: The World indicates that Nick's past career was a successful and rewarding one, in which he had the world at his feet. Now he has to be patient and give up the old ways of thinking, feeling and doing. He has to act from a fresh mindset and his newly found vocation will be a successful and abundant one. He will enjoy interacting and communicating with clients and people around him. To clarify further what he has to give up, we follow the second card by choosing another major card, Strength, which indicates his inner strength and abilities are infinite. By taming 'the beast within' he will move forward gently and assuredly.

EXAMPLES OF THREE-CARD SPREADS		
CARD 1	CARD 2	CARD 3
Past	Present	Future
Body	Mind	Spirit
Subconscious	Conscious	Higher wisdom
Child	Parent	Adult
The nature of the problem	The cause of the problem	Advice
Problem	Action	Outcome
The idea	Criticism of it	How to improve it
(Add your own here)	(Add your own here)	(Add your own here)

Figure 20: Ideas for a three-card spread

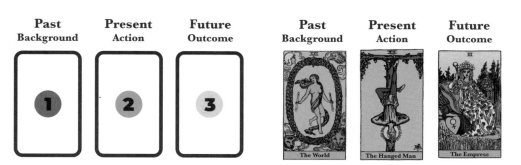

Past Background	**Present** Action	**Future** Outcome
1	**2**	**3**

Figure 21:
Layout for a three-card spread

The Yes-Or-No Spread

Use this spread when you require a straightforward yes-or-no response, because the answer hangs in the balance. The Justice card is placed in the background as a reminder for a decisive outcome. If the outcome is indecisive, follow by picking an additional card to clarify it further. Please refer to Figure 19 for cards to be followed. If your question is about the outcome of a legal issue, you can place the Judgement card as a background, instead of Justice.

SAMPLE READING: Lucy is a consultant who was approached by a company to work on a new project. A verbal agreement was reached and she was asked to begin working on this project with the contract to follow. Although she has already started working on this project, she has not heard from that company since.

QUESTION: 'What is the outcome of the project Lucy has in mind?'

CARDS IN THE SPREAD: Background – The Tower, Turning Point – The World, Outcome – The Moon followed by Strength.

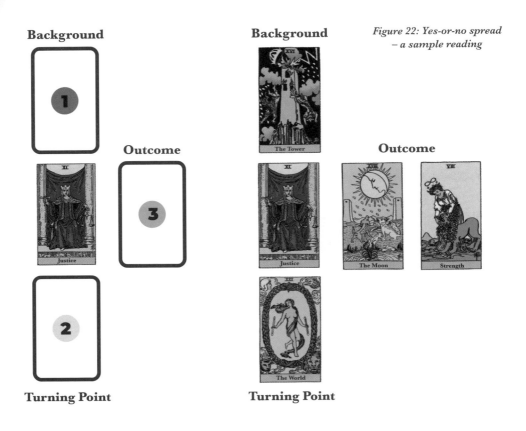

Background

Outcome

2

Turning Point

Background

*Figure 22: Yes-or-no spread
– a sample reading*

Outcome

Turning Point

INTERPRETATION: This project proposal came to Lucy all of a sudden (The Tower) and, although she was not expecting it, it shows great promise of fulfilling her ambition (The World). The Moon denotes that, although she feels emotional and uncertain about signing a contract, she needs to follow her intuition and continue. Strength indicates that the project will end well. Her inner strength will help her overcome her doubts. She needs to trust the process of issuing that contract.

The Five-Card Star Spread

When you want guidance around an issue and to know the best course of action for a favourable outcome, the five-card spread fits that purpose. As the name suggests, the layout follows the formation of a star where card 1 denotes the problem, card 2 is the cause, card 3 represents the underlying factors, card 4 signifies the best course of action or proposed advice and, finally, card 5 highlights the result or outcome, if you follow the advice given.

Sometimes, when you are reading for others, they may wish not to disclose what their questions are. In that case, you phrase the question: 'What about the issue X has in mind?' Very often, the first card in the five-card star spread will let you know what the nature of the problem is.

SAMPLE READING: Sofia has been on her own since she lost her long-term partner a few years ago. Several months ago, she made a new friend and is confused about the nature of this relationship and her feelings.

QUESTION: 'What about the relationship between Sofia and her new friend?'

CARDS IN THE SPREAD:

Card 1 – The Problem: The nature of the problem in question is a relationship. The Lovers card is reversed, indicating that romance will not transpire. This relationship could simply be about friendship.

Card 2 – The Cause: The Hermit indicates that the enquirer, Sofia, was on her own for a while. This period of being alone can offer her space to reflect, learn more about herself, readjust before she is in a relationship again, and find a higher meaning to her past experience. Her loneliness is the cause of confused feelings.

Card 3 – Factors: She is going through a transition phase of rebirth, which is not over. She probably needs time and space on her own to figure things out. The Death card here also indicates that the situation between them will change. It denotes the death of uncertainty and a birth, or new beginning, where she will know exactly how she feels, and the end of being on her own.

Card 4 – Advice: The Empress is about beauty and abundance. Her advice is for Sofia to be happy, joyful, look after herself and reconnect or socialise with supportive friends whose company she enjoys – perhaps even to get a makeover.

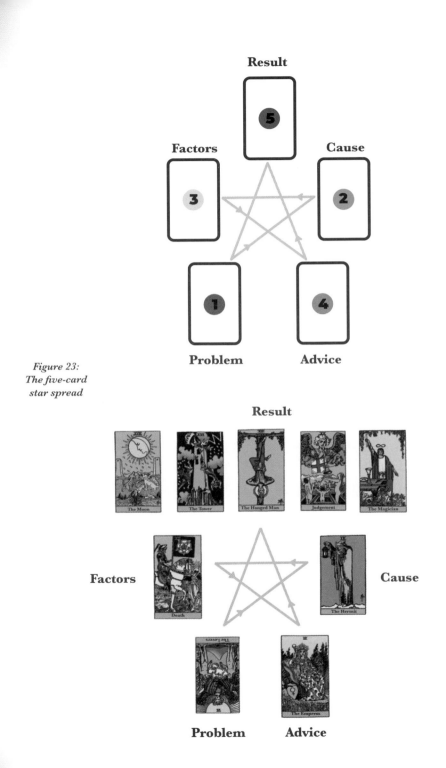

Figure 23:
The five-card
star spread

Card 5 – Result: The first result card is The Moon, followed by a series of cards until a definite answer is reached. They are as follows: The Tower, The Hanged Man, Judgement and, finally, The Magician.

The Moon denotes uncertainty and lack of clarity, as well as an emotional state. Through surrendering and trusting that 'all will be clear' in time, Sofia can also ask for guidance in her dreams. The Tower indicates a sudden change of circumstance. However, The Hanged Man indicates that Sofia needs this period of reflection to develop a higher perspective. Judgement confirms that she is going through a significant transformation, and that this period of seemingly enforced loneliness is necessary to help her reinvent her life and prepare for the new cycle of rebirthing. The final result card, The Magician, indicates that all will end well. She has the resources within her to overcome this difficult period and transition into a new successful phase of her life. Moreover, communication between the couple will become clearer as they meet as friends, since this relationship is more learning about herself than about starting a romance.

OVERALL INTERPRETATION: Although Sofia's question was about the nature of a new friendship, the cards revealed that the situation was more about her developing understanding of the transition period she is going through. Her loneliness caused her to think of this friendship as a possibility for romance, but, instead, it is helping her to reinvent herself and her life. In the meantime, she is called upon to reunite with other friends. It is not time for romance, but rather a reflective period of healing and preparing for the next cycle of her life. A new beginning is on the horizon and this uncertainty will end.

The 12-House Astrological Spread

Based on the 12 houses of the zodiac, the 12-house astrological spread is suitable for an annual overall reading to see trends over long-term future. It is also appropriate for someone who has not had a reading before. The layout of the spread is similar to an astrological birth chart, but the 12 houses are arranged in two rows of six houses each. This simplifies the interpretations of cards in the

12-house layout, and provides additional possibilities of these interpretations (see sample reading below).

Once you have shuffled the major cards and reversed two cards, randomly choose 12 cards, one at a time, and place each in the order of the 12 houses. Later, when you are more confident with the tarot interpretation, you can extend this spread by shuffling the minor cards (reversing five cards) and selecting 12 cards, one over each house respectively as in Figure 25.

You can also draw an additional 13th card to represent the outcome of the reading. Note the number of the card. Adding the numerological interpretation to your reading provides further perspective. The cards are interpreted according to the attributes of each of the 12 astrological houses they fall into, as below in Figure 24.

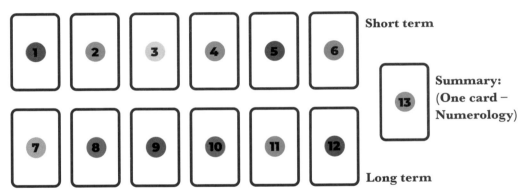

Figure 24: The 12-house astrological spread

1	Aries Mars	THE SELF	Personality and temperament of the enquirer at the time of the reading.
2	Taurus Venus	INCOME	A person's ability to earn income and material possessions, how they are earning and their attitude to money.
3	Gemini Mercury	COMMUNICATION	Conscious thoughts at the time of the reading, mental abilities and state, communication with other people, writing, travel, short journeys.

4	Cancer Moon	HOME LIFE	Physical home and physical body (abode of the soul). Type of influences around the home, property transactions.
5	Leo Sun	LOVE/ROMANCE	Love/Romance. Marriage, creative expression, talents, affairs, pregnancy and children.
6	Virgo Mercury	PHYSICAL HEALTH	Work habits, co-workers, healing potential, recovering from illness, daily routine, diet, service to others.
7	Libra Venus	PARTNERSHIPS	Business and romantic partnerships, permanent or committed unions.
8	Scoprio Pluto	CRISIS/ TRANSITIONS	State of shared finances (spouse, business partner). Tax, sex, death (physical or death of old self, be careful with interpreting death, other cards need to be present in houses 1, 4 and 6). Beginnings and endings.
9	Sagittarius Jupiter	LEGAL MATTERS	Long journeys, legal contracts, people from overseas. Background, philosophy in life, the future.
10	Capricorn Saturn	WORK/AMBITION	Success in career, work environment; how your community sees you.
11	Aquarius Uranus	NEXT CYCLE/ SOCIAL LIFE	Goals in life, hopes and aspirations, friends and social activities, group aspiration, humanitarian and creative endeavours.
12	Pieces Neptune	THE SUBCONSCIOUS	Fears, limitations, beginning of the next new cycle, hidden enemies.
13		OVERALL OUTCOME	The theme of the overall spread.

m	m	m	m	m	m

1ST HOUSE	2ND HOUSE	3RD HOUSE	4TH HOUSE	5TH HOUSE	6TH HOUSE
Aries – Mars	Taurus – Venus	Gemini – Mercury	Cancer – Moon	Leo – Sun	Virgo – Mercury
THE SELF	MONEY	COMMUNICATION	HOME LIFE	LOVE/ ROMANCE	HEALTH
The present state of mind	Current income	Short term future, journeys, mindset	Domestic life, physical body	Creativity, talent, children	Healing, employment, co-workers

M	M	M	M	M	M

M	M	M	M	M	M

PARTNERSHIPS	TRANSITIONS	LEGAL MATTERS	CAREER AMBITION	NEXT CYCLE	SUBCONSCIOUS
Business and marriage partnerships	Shared finances, taxes, inheritance, sex	Long term future, higher education, overseas journeys	Work conditions, success	Social activities, friends, aspirations	Inner feelings, limiting thoughts, fears, worries, dreams
7TH HOUSE	8TH HOUSE	9TH HOUSE	10TH HOUSE	11TH HOUSE	12TH HOUSE
Libra – Venus	Scorpio – Pluto	Sagittarius – Jupiter	Capricorn – Saturn	Aquarius – Uranus	Pieces – Neptune

m	m	m	m	m	m

Figure 25: The 12-house astrological spread with the minor cards

Moreover, spreading the 12 houses over two rows allows you to relate cards in the top row to cards in the bottom. For example, the 1st house is the ascendant to the 7th house below it, the descendant; the 2nd house, of the ability to earn money, is ascendant to the 8th house, the state of your finances, and so on.

Once you lay the cards out, allow the images on the cards to inspire your interpretation. If you like, a simpler way is to see the top row as the present or short-term future and the second row as the long-term outcome of each of the houses in the top row.

House Combinations

The 12-house astrological spread is a good template for the tarot to tell a story. So, the next thing you consider, once you have completed laying out the cards, is house combinations to see how the story unfolds. For example, Lovers in the 5th house denotes the potential of a relationship. You then look at the 7th house (partnerships) and the 9th house (legal matters) to see if this relationship is going to lead to marriage. If health is a concern, or when the person you are reading for is enquiring about their health, you consider the 1st house (the self), the 4th house (physical body) and the 6th house (healing) to see how they are recovering. Furthermore, if the health situation is critical, consider the 8th house to see the outcome of transformation.

Other house combinations to look for are career development – the 2nd + 6th +10th – the ability to earn money, work environment and promotions, respectively. And when you are considering personal growth and transformation, consider the 8th and 12th, which represent the end of the old and the beginning of a new phase and how that phase will transpire as indicated in the 12th house, which denotes the next new cycle (see Figure 26 for house combinations).

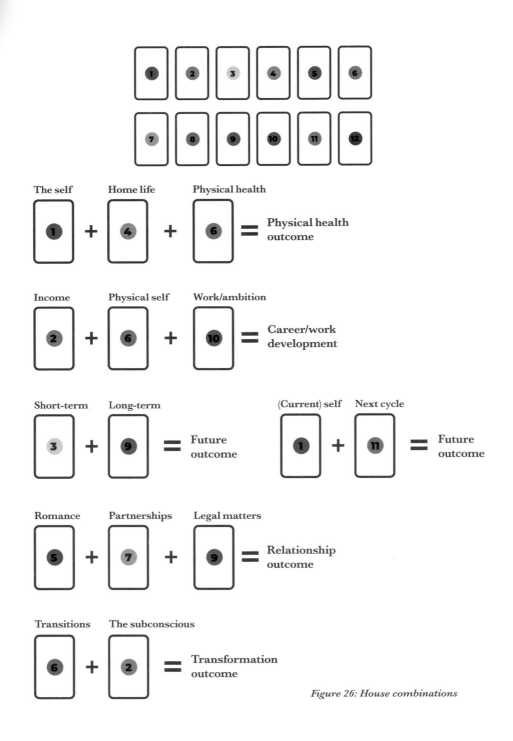

Figure 26: House combinations

SAMPLE READING: Ranya is approaching 50, and is concerned about what the future holds for her, her husband and her health. She feels unsure about what decisions to make, and what direction to take in life, particularly to enhance her experience of life.

QUESTIONS: 'What are the important changes happening now in Ranya's life and in her long-term future?'

Starting a full reading by considering the date of birth of the enquirer, as well as the tarot spread, is a great way to tune into their life purpose and correlate insights from numerology and the tarot. Her Birthforce/Life Path number is 5, indicating she is destined to fulfil her life's ambitions on her own terms, by freeing herself from preconceived ideas and usual ways of thinking.

However, her path may not always be clear because it seems to be going through constant transformation. It is because of this constant transformation (21 into 3) that her talents will expand, and her life will financially thrive. The number 5 operates on a higher level and is about the need to engage your intuition and higher wisdom. Moreover, number 5s have a need for stimulation, if they stay too long in a dissatisfying situation, their impulse is to leave it, seeking change in order to grow.

Ranya's core essence is 10, revealing a heightened talent and ability for communication, marketing and starting her own business, following her own guidance (2) and doing things her way (5). What she yearns for is the freedom to travel (7) and the ability to transcend all obstacles, which she will achieve by mastering her mind and staying connected to her own source of inspiration, like The Chariot who moves forward once he realises what the obstacle is.

Her challenge in this life is to trust her intuition and act on what she feels is true to her heart. Subtle guidance will be received through her dreams. Additionally, her personal year, at the time of the reading (pre 1st October), is a 7, emphasising that this year is all about learning to master her mindset, talents and skills, and that next year would be ideal for her to manifest her dreams (8) into material success, having understood the spiritual laws of bringing ideas into reality. Moreover, for number 8 is about the ability to be stable in endeavours and avoid fluctuating between gain and loss, she has to maintain her balance by staying connected with what is in her heart.

RANYA'S DATE OF BIRTH: 1 October 1974

$1 + (1 + 0 = 1) + (1 + 9 + 7 + 4 = 21) = 2 + 1 = 3 = 1 + 1 + 3$
$= 5$

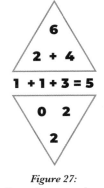

Figure 27:
Ranya's numerology triangle

UNDERLYING INFLUENCE IN 2022:

$2 + 2022 = 2 + 6 = 8$, so current underlying influences $= 8$, which will start from her birthday in 2022. If it is before her birthday, she is a 7 moving into 8.

CARDS IN THE SPREAD: See Figure 28 opposite. Let's consider the 1st, 12th and 13th cards of the 12-house astrological spread. The card in the 1st house tells Ranya that the capable, creative Queen of Wands is bearing the brunt of making decisions about the next phase of her life, feeling muddled, as though she can't stand on her own feet (The Lovers reversed)! However, the cards in the 7th house indicate that both partners will achieve what they hope for, The Star indicates the support and love of her husband, and that they will both experience a blissful life together. The 2 of Wands denotes a successful partnership and expansion, perhaps abroad.

The 12th card, The Empress, shows that by the start of her new cycle she will have conquered her fears and self-belief about money, health and abundance. This success is confirmed further by the 3 of Cups, indicating that she will have a great deal to celebrate, giving birth to a new way of life.

The 13th card, The Hermit, summarises the spread, confirming that this year is about deepening her spiritual understanding and seeking higher knowledge. She probably needs to give herself time and space to explore, through reflection and meditation, for example. Her journey will inspire by example (The Hermit lights the way for others).

Ranya will be able to generate income from her talents and abilities as The Chariot indicates in the 2nd house. So, she does not lack in skills or abilities, but perhaps needs to make more effort in mastering their expression in her own unique way. It also denotes that she could be successful earning money through travel, or travel writing (Ace of Pentacles). Cards in the 8th house indicate Ranya is worried

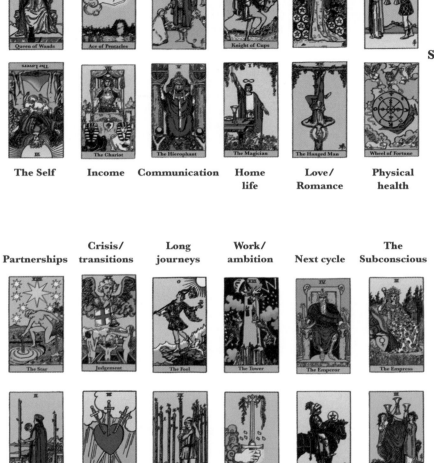

Short term

The Self   Income   Communication   Home life   Love/ Romance   Physical health

Partnerships   Crisis/ transitions   Long journeys   Work/ ambition   Next cycle   The Subconscious

Summary

Long term

Figure 28: A 12-house sample reading

about the state of their shared finances, her husband is disappointed too (3 of Swords), and Judgement indicates that their finances are unsettled but that both of them should put their heads together and share the decisions on how to create a new way of earning money through their talents. The absence of the Justice card in houses 5, 6 and 8 indicates that their income will not be through a job, but rather through levelling up their skills, abilities and talents, establishing an independent way to express them.

The Hierophant, and 6 of Pentacles, in the 3rd house convey that if Ranya trusts her own intuition, she will be supported in sustaining her income. She could be earning money from communicating her own ideas, in other words, through writing. Now, consider the cards in the 9th house – the long-term outcome. The Fool indicates that there is a long journey ahead, taking a risk in a move to a new country, perhaps. Also, the idea of using her mind and writing skills in a new way is what she is struggling with. Ranya needs to drop all her worries (9 of Wands) and listen to her own guidance (The Hierophant). When the time comes, she will know exactly what to do.

The 4th house denotes that Ranya is – or will be – working from home. Again, The Magician, confirms that her talents are to do with her mind and communication. The Knight of Cups represents her partner, whom she shares a home with, and that he too is working, or can work, from home. When you look at cards in the 10th house, you see The Tower, indicating that work will suddenly change and that she will taking a decision (Ace of Swords) to do so.

Cards in the 5th house indicate that Ranya's creative talents will transform, taking a different expression (The Hanged Man), which is probably why this period is a frustrating one in which nothing seems to be happening. However, the 9 of Pentacles indicates that she could be successful at creating her own independent writing platform. The Emperor in the 11th house shows that she will achieve her hopes and aspirations by staying focused and working on them. An older experienced man, who is good with finances (Knight of Pentacles), might offer advice and support her in achieving them.

The Wheel of Fortune in the 6th house also shows there is a change in career soon, and that she and her partner will have something to celebrate (2 of Cups).

Cards in the 12th house indicate that this change will affect her partner too, indicating that he may have something to celebrate as the way he works changes.

When you look at the cards that showed up in Ranya's reading, you will notice several Pentacle cards, indicating that finances will be all right. The positive Cup cards indicate happiness and celebration; the Swords indicate disappointment leading to decision-making. They also give an overall impression that there is a need for the couple to consider going independent with their work. Both are talented and skilled; however, they are advised to shift their mindset from worry to action, share the decision-making, and support each other in taking a risk towards something new, such as a move abroad. The frustration indicates a transformation into a new way of abundant living.

Finally, regarding the question about health, consider the cards in houses 1, 4, 6, 8 and 12. The Lovers reversed in the 1st house signifies the need for both partners to make a change in their diet soon. The Magician card in the 4th house demonstrates that they are both living in a comfortable home which is conducive for the growth of their talents, as well as their health. The Wheel of Fortune, in the 6th house, indicates they can both achieve balance quickly. Judgement in the 8th house signifies a health crisis if weight issues are not addressed soon. The Empress in the 12th house indicates they can both achieve their health goals successfully.

Closing thoughts

The tarot started its journey as a set of cards to play tricks, games and entertain. It fired the imagination of the various cultures it travelled through, becoming increasingly popular – so much so that each added its own input until the cards became the tarot we know today. The tarot can be considered a 'game' that helps you to find out the answers to your life's journey. We hope that you will have the courage of our hero, The Fool, and that this book will help you to find the wisdom and support you need to live your life as fearlessly as he did.

Further Reading

Create Your Own Flower Tarot – Sahar Hunedi-Palmer

Tarot – Alice Ekrek

Intuitive Tarot – Brigit Esselmont

The Ultimate Guide to the Tarot – Johannes Fiebig

Seventy-eight Degrees of Wisdom – Rachel Pollack

The Pictorial Key to the Tarot – A.E. Waite

Author online

Website: www.saharhuneidi.com

Twitter: @saharhuneidi

Podcast: Unbox The Podcast: Live Your Best Life with Sahar

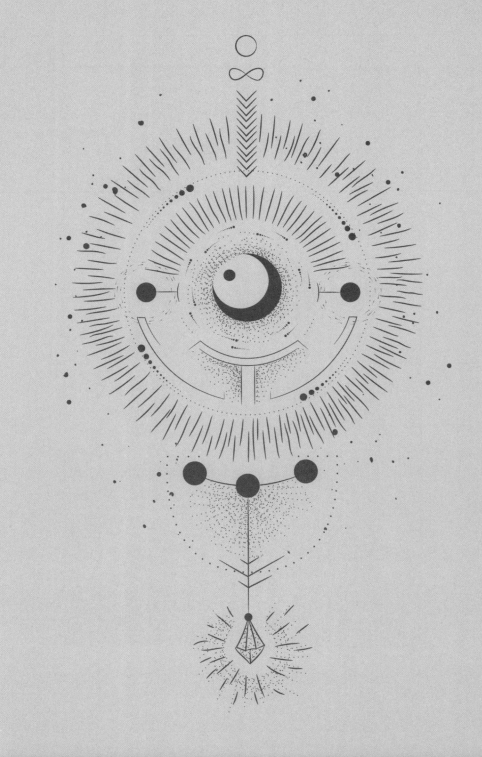